GRÍMSEY

ÓLAFSFJARÐARMÚLI

SKORUVÍKUR-
BJARG
SKORUVÍK
SAUÐANES †
ÞÓRSHÖFN
GUNNÓLFSVÍKURFJALL

ÞINGEYJARSÝSLUR

VOPNAFJÖRÐUR
VOPNAFJÖRÐUR
HELLIS-
HEIÐI

VESTURÁRDALUR
SELÁ
REFSTAÐUR II

MÝVATN
MÖÐRUDALUR †
SUNNUDALUR
SMÖRFJÖLL

AKUREYRI
FNJÓSKADALUR
BÁRÐARDALUR

SVARTÁRVATN
SVARTÁRKOT
EGILSSTAÐIR

MJÓIDALUR
ÓDÁÐAHRAUN
HERÐUBREIÐ
JÖKULDALUR
SKRÚÐUR

ASKJA
ÖSKJUVATN
DYNGJUFJÖLL

PAPEY

ÓFS-
KULL
BÁRÐAR-
BUNGA

VATNAJÖKULL

ICELAND

THE WINDO

AN AMERI

THE WINDOWS OF BRIMNES

AN AMERICAN IN ICELAND

BILL HOLM

MILKWEED EDITIONS

Published 2007 by Milkweed Editions
Printed in Canada
Cover design by Christian Fünfhausen
Cover photo by Thorsten Henn,
  Nordicphotos.com
Author photo by Einar Falur
Interior design by Wendy Holdman
The text of this book is set in Warnock.
07 08 09 10 11 6 5 4 3 2 1
First Edition

Milkweed Editions, a nonprofit publisher, gratefully acknowledges sustaining support from Emilie and Henry Buchwald; the Bush Foundation; the Patrick and Aimee Butler Family Foundation; CarVal Investors; the Timothy and Tara Clark Family Charitable Fund; the Dougherty Family Foundation; the Ecolab Foundation; the General Mills Foundation; the Claire Giannini Fund; John and Joanne Gordon; William and Jeanne Grandy; the Jerome Foundation; Dorothy Kaplan Light and Ernest Light; Constance B. Kunin; Marshall BankFirst Corp.; Sanders and Tasha Marvin; the May Department Stores Company Foundation; the McKnight Foundation; a grant from the Minnesota State Arts Board, through an appropriation by the Minnesota State Legislature, a grant from the National Endowment for the Arts, and private funders; an award from the National Endowment for the Arts, which believes that a great nation deserves great art; the Navarre Corporation; Debbie Reynolds; the St. Paul Travelers Foundation; Ellen and Sheldon Sturgis; the Target Foundation; the Gertrude Sexton Thompson Charitable Trust (George R. A. Johnson, Trustee); the James R. Thorpe Foundation; the Toro Foundation; Moira and John Turner; United Parcel Service; Joanne and Phil Von Blon; Kathleen and Bill Wanner; Serene and Christopher Warren; the W. M. Foundation; and the Xcel Energy Foundation.

Milkweed would like to acknowledge the following permissions:

"Watering the Horse" from *Eating the Honey of Words* (New York, NY: HarperCollins, 1999). Copyright © 1999 by Robert Bly. Reprinted with permission from Robert Bly.

"All Quiet" from *Against the Evidence: Selected Poems 1934–1994* (Middletown, CT: Wesleyan University Press, 1994). Copyright © 1968 by David Ignatow. Reprinted with permission from Wesleyan University Press (www.wesleyan.edu/wespress).

"The Silent Piano" from *The Owner of the House* (Rochester, NY: BOA Editions, 2003). Copyright © 1971 by Louis Simpson. Reprinted with permission from BOA Editions (www. boaeditions.org).

"At the Un-National Monument along the Canadian Border" from *The Way It Is* (St. Paul, Minn.: Graywolf Press, 1998). Copyright © 1975, 1998 by the Estate of William Stafford. Reprinted with permission from Graywolf Press (www.graywolfpress.org).

Library of Congress Cataloging-in-Publication Data

Holm, Bill, 1943–
The windows of Brimnes : an American in Iceland / Bill Holm. — 1st ed.
  p. cm.
ISBN 978-1-57131-302-7
  (acid-free paper)
1. Americans—Iceland. 2. Iceland—Description and travel. 3. United States.
I. Title.
PS3558.O3558W56 2007
811'.54—dc22 2007022209

                                          CIP

This book is printed on acid-free paper.

MINNESOTA
STATE ARTS BOARD

NATIONAL
ENDOWMENT
FOR THE ARTS

For Kristján Árnason, poet, carpenter, maker of beauty from wood and words, a representative type of the Icelandic farmer-intellectual who refused to let either isolation or poverty keep him from practicing his art.

THE WINDOWS OF BRIMNES

AN AMERICAN IN ICELAND

No book is ever made without the wisdom and generosity of friends. I list them as the alphabet finds them. A thousand thanks.

David Arnason
Kristján Árnason
Margret and Örn Arnar
Sverrir Ásgrímsson
Fred Bjarnason
Carol Bly
Robert Bly
Marcy Brekken
Emilie Buchwald
Nelson Gerrard
Daren Gíslason
Hallgrímur Gunnarsson
Tom Guttormsson
Margret Kólka Haraldsdottir
Jón Baldvin Hannibalsson
Anna Sigga Helgadóttir
Víðar Hreinsson
Wincie Jóhannsdottir
Áslaug Jónsdottir
Cathy Josephson
Charles and Joan Josephson
Les and Donna Josephson
Jón Magnusson
Gail Perrizo
David Pichaske
Bryndís Schram

John and Lorna Rezmerski
Dagmar Ásdis Þorvaldsdottir
Þórnalur Þorvaldsson
Valgeir Þorvaldsson
Doris and Don Wenig

And of course,

Daniel Slager
Hilary Reeves
Emily Cook
Patrick Thomas
Jim Cihlar

And the whole gang at
Milkweed Editions

With particular thanks to the
Icelandic translation squad:

Wincie Jóhannsdottir
Margret Arnar
Margret Kólka Haraldsdottir
Wallgrímur Gunnarsson
Nelson Gerrard
Áslaug Jónsdottir

THE WINDOWS OF BRIMNES

AN AMERICAN IN ICELAND

BRIMNES: NAME AND PLACE

In the summer of 2001, a journalist from St. Paul, Minnesota, a young woman with a sense of adventure, decided to spend a week touring Iceland. I invited her to stop by and see me in Hofsós. There's no address, I said. There are only a few hundred people, and they will all know how to find the crazy American. Just ask for Brimnes. I'm next to the sea. And if you can't find the sea, you're out of luck.

She landed at Keflavík International Airport at 6:00 A.M., rented a car, and decided to drive straight north. She found Highway 1, Esja, the tunnel, the pass, even the country music station, and finally the turn off Highway 1 to Hofsós. The sun shone grandly. Wildflowers bloomed dependably in the ditches, the motor purred, and the sight of the sea and the mountains helped stave off the jet lag.

She drove north with open windows and a glad heart. Soon a drink, lunch, a nap, a friendly and familiar American face. Suddenly she hit the brakes and stopped, ten miles south of Hofsós. By the side of the road was a blue metal sign: ← *Brimnes*. It pointed toward the fjord to the east. He hadn't said whether he lived right in town. This must be it. She turned west down a long gravel driveway, passed through a gate which she responsibly closed behind her, and arrived at a farmstead with a real barn, a corral of horses, a stack of hay bales wrapped in plastic, a tractor, but an empty yard. So he's bought a farm, she thought, and got out to stretch her legs. Out from the barn came a young farmer in black rubber boots and a blood-soaked slicker. Behind him trotted his five- or six-year-old daughter, same rubber boots, same slicker, but smaller, carrying a bleeding sheep's head.

"Is this Brimnes?" asked a now-confused Amy.

"Brimnes? Já. Þetta er Brimnes," said the farmer, clearly astonished at the sound of English, a language he probably neither speaks nor understands and also not the lingua franca of the neighborhood. The little girl with the sheep's head examined the pretty young foreigner in the shiny rental car. "Go to the house and fetch your mother," said the farmer in Icelandic to his daughter. "She understands a little English."

Soon the mother emerged, wiping floury hands on her apron. Amy explained again that she was looking for Bill Holm, an American living at Brimnes. "Oh, not this Brimnes," said the mother in halting English. "Kannski hann býr in town Hofsós, fifteen kilometers north. Brimnes there too, I think."

Amy thanked the family in her best English, apologizing, with her sweetest American smile, for interrupting the sheep butchering, and drove back down the way she came, carefully closing the gate behind her. Fifteen minutes later she found me, not in Brimnes but rather at the end of a telephone line. She'd stopped at the little general store (the only store in Hofsós), and when she inquired after Bill Holm, Dagný, the blond clerk and postmistress's daughter, told her I was probably having coffee down at the Icelandic Emigration Center, but that she'd ring there and track me down. All this, much to Amy's relief, in fluent English. I was summoned to the phone. "Did you have a good trip up? You must be half-dead of jet lag."

"I had a little adventure," said Amy.

"Such is life in Iceland. One of its great pleasures, in fact."

This had been Amy's first experience with the Icelanders' habit of naming every farm, every house, and of course every rock, rise, gully, and bay in this mostly empty landscape. *Brim* means waves or surf breaking on the beach, *nes* means cape, promontory, or headland, thus Brimnes—a miniature peninsula. Most of the country lives within spitting distance of salt water, which means there must be at least fifty Brimneses scattered over all districts of Iceland. Names repeat themselves endlessly: a hundred *Hrauns* (lava); farms called *Vatn* (lake or water), *Bær* (farmstead), *Brú* (bridge), and *Ós* (river's mouth). The local trolls worship at many churches: the mountain *Tröllakirkja*. Or perhaps they dine at the west fjord rocks called *Trollasamlokur*—"troll sandwiches." And as with places, so with humans. I was once kissed by eight Guðrúns in one night, and shook hands with a dozen Björns. Are Americans short of Johns and Marys?

Without a name, does a place exist? And what is the right name? And who is the right giver of names? Iceland is, if not the last, one of the few countries in the world to use a system of patronymics, in which the first name is the real identifier and the last only a temporary convenience used to establish connections between generations. If you wish to find a Guðrún or a Björn in Iceland, you must consult the telephone directory by first name. You may find twenty Guðrún Björnsdóttirs in Reykjavík alone. Start ringing at the top of the list. Good luck. Eventually one of the Guðrúns will know the one you are looking for and provide you with the right number. With 300,000-odd Icelanders, anonymity may be completely impossible. An American can disappear and invent a new name, a new identity, but don't try it in Iceland. Someone will know. . . .

Houses in country villages have names as well. Many farms have had the same name for a thousand years, even if the existing turf house has actually been built upon the remains of another. After all, it has been the same old *Höfði* (headland) since 974.

"Ah, Friðrik from Höfði—just north of Vatn and south of Lónkot."

"Ah, you have bought Brimnes. Björn Björnsson, the doctor, was born there. Eight children grew up in that tiny house. Their father was a fisherman—so handy to the harbor."

"You know Sölvi Helgason lived at Skálá the last few years of his life. Died in—what?—1895. Never could get along with the sheriff's daughter who owned the farm. Friðrik Þór owns it now."

"You know a great poet once lived at Sléttuhlíð. When? The eighteenth century."

These names comprise a *sveit*—a word, according to my friend Elva Friðriksdóttir, untranslatable into English. The dictionary mumbles about "country, neighborhood, rural district, municipality, community, parish . . . ," but when she talks about her sveit, Elva does not slap her forehead or stomp her foot. She strikes her heart. Sveit is what connects you to the earth, to history, to nature, to humanity.

Elva's sveit begins at her father's farm, Höfði, where Guðríður Þorbjarnardóttir settled in about AD 1000 with her husband, Þórfinnur Karlsefni, and their son Snorri—the first European conceived and born in the New World, Vinland. The farmhouse at Höfði was built, not of turf but rather of timber, about 1900 (a long life for an Icelandic farmhouse). Elva's father, Friðrik, keeps it intact, though he's built a comfortable and modern house a few hundred feet away. Intact old farmhouses are so rare in Iceland these days that his nephew Friðrik Þór, one of Iceland's best film directors, has used the old house as a movie set three or four times. Just across the road, the narrow gravel spit leads a half mile into the sea to connect the seven-hundred-foot cliff of Þórðarhöfði to the mainland. That thin spit is a good metaphor for what connects the many Elvas and Friðriks of Iceland to their sveit—it's invisible from even five miles away, from where Þórðarhöfði looks like an island, but always visible to those who know it's there.

Is sveit an impossible notion for Americans, with our tiny history, our broken connections to any past, our indifference to nature (if money is to be made), our internal itchiness to keep moving and reinvent ourselves? An old friend of mine in Minnesota who used to live on a lake miles from any village now lives not at the old Peterson place, or at RR #2, Hawk Lake, but at 15631 469th Ave. SE in the nearest market town of over ten thousand. No use giving his house a name, since the post only arrives with a minimum of twenty anonymous numbers. There are too many of us, and we are too hard to keep track of. We like to put things in numerical order, in case the authorities should need us suddenly.

After the horrors of September 11, Americans became obsessed with security—internal security, or, to use the sentimental euphemism, homeland security. Yet if we examine our true perceptions without fear of hysteria, almost everyone knows that thumbprints, hidden cameras, scanners, national ID's, armed national guards, wiretaps, X-rayed shoes, and other draconian invasions of personal privacy cannot make us safe. Handing over vast power to a secret police apparatus will not allow us to sleep more soundly in our personal beds or to attend to our daily business without fear. True civilization, true security, depends on a level of trust between neighbors that Americans seem willing to barter away at the summons of any skillful sloganeer.

Neighbors know each other's names. They know not only the houses but also the history of the houses in their sveit: "The Van Keulens moved out to the old Josephson farm—not J.A.'s—it was S. Frank's dad, Árni, who built that house." They know one another's children and welcome them into their houses, not to protect them from dangerous strangers but to feed them, pat them on the head, or keep them out of the tomatoes. Does this seem cockamamie foolishness to you—some sentimental voice from a long-lost golden age? If so, then our sense of civility has fallen into such disrepair that not even fifty trillion dollars' worth of electronic guard gizmos and internal security forces can save us.

Not only are we too many, we make our vast numbers worse by clumping. Even worse, we swear fealty to our companies, our employers, rather than to our neighbors. The hand that signs your check (or the electronic substitute for that hand) is not your friend nor your neighbor, no matter how many cheerful greetings or "nice days" it wishes you. On the other hand, your neighbor Bob, who dislikes you, probably wishes that a truck would back into your Chevy or that you'd sprain your ankle in the unfilled pothole in the sidewalk. That, though, is a far friendlier and safer gesture than any anonymous institution will ever give you. At least Bob does not mean to murder you anonymously with some sort of newly invented bomb. Anonymous murder is the vilest of all assaults on civilization. Kill Bob if you please; that's human. Just be sure to take the trouble to find out his shoe size and his mother's maiden name before you do it. Otherwise, leave him alone to stew in his own life.

So, having now been properly harangued on the subjects of anonymity and neighborliness, you should begin to discern not only the physical but the psychological virtue of living in a properly named house. Having arrived, like Amy, at the right Brimnes, you should know something of the house, its history, its architecture, its neighbors, its location on the planet, and what can be seen out its windows.

I first saw Hofsós because a choir-mate of an old friend was working there as Director of the Vesturfarasetrið (the Icelandic Emigration Center). A carload of friends arrived on a sunny

June midafternoon, the season of endless light. We met Dísa
(Vigdís Esradóttir, soprano and Director of the Center). We
met Valgeir Þorvaldsson, the impresario of Hofsós who had
conceived the notion of a museum and genealogy center in his
collapsing though beautiful hometown—his sveit. Farming and
fishing no longer keep the district children from disappearing
into Reykjavík, or abroad. It is the same, endless story of small,
out-of-the-way places. It is the same in America, in Canada, in
Europe, and all over the planet: who wants to live in the boondocks, even beautiful boondocks? Even if those boondocks
are your sveit? Valgeir, a carpenter by training and inclination,
had worked for the county on a couple of historical projects
and had now begun buying old, half-collapsed fisherman's cot-
tages set helter-skelter on a lumpy hillside above the mouth of
the Hof River. At the top of the steep little hill, a newer, more
modern concrete town had grown up. A few businesses: bank,
post office, garage, cooperative store, church, school, community hall, soccer field, and muffler factory. Just another dying
small place, thirty miles off the main road.

The original village at the bottom of the hill consisted of
fifteen or twenty unmatched houses in various states of re-
pair. Some had been moved there from another site a half mile
south, where yet another noisy glacial river, the Grafará, had
made a little, sheltered nest of grass at its mouth—now only a
few ruined lumps and cavities carpeted with wildflowers. The
two sites were thousand-year-old Viking trading posts for the
north fjords, and had been a single named village since the sixteenth century. The Viking longboats would bring their goods
to anchor at the river's mouth and trade with the local farmers for dried fish, hides, wool, and smoked meat. Books must
have been traded, too, and then carried to the rest of Iceland
by water. The first printing press in the country was ten miles

away in the prosperous Hólar Valley, site of the northern episcopate of Iceland.

The little fishing harbor on the north side of the river's mouth has been much improved over the centuries, with the addition of a stone breakwater, regular dredging, and a clearly marked channel. Still, at the outset of the twenty-first century, just four fishing boats called it home—and only one of them was large enough (or in possession of enough valuable fish quotas) to provide a true living. Yet the fjord itself has long been chockablock with cod, along with a nice scattering of haddock, halibut, catfish, and sea trout. At the top of the gravel road going up the hill to the north of the harbor sat a fish-salting station, barrels of cod on their way to becoming twenty-five-dollar-a-plate *bacalao* served with a coulis of tomatoes and peppers *a la Español*.

The sveit still kept intact its old economic resources—the sea harvest; the rich, grassy meadows that nourished the sheep and dairy cattle; the cream of Icelandic horse stocks; the cliffs abundant with eggs and tasty seabirds. The neighbors were literate and kindly, and there were overstuffed bookshelves in almost every house. There were local singers of high repute and skill, and even local writers who published small volumes of well-made, old-fashioned verse. One of them, an unschooled carpenter who wrote well in three languages—Icelandic, English, and Danish—had won literary prizes in Reykjavík newspapers.

All this and the majesty out every window: huge mountains, the multicolored sea, the glaciers, noisy rivers surging fjord-ward over a bed of symmetrical columnar basalt, the cliffs, the decorator islands, the wildflowers and sweet grass in season, not to mention the three-month-long daylight. If you had to choose a sveit, this would be a tempting possibility. But usually a sveit chooses you, and so it had chosen

Valgeir—thus he carpentered away on the old houses, then put on his necktie to go raise funds from government, business, immigrant groups from North America, anybody who might stock Skagafjörður with cash enough to keep this sveit alive and flourishing.

My wife, Marcy, and I slept in Brimnes on our first night in Hofsós. At the time it was a small guest house with four Lilliputian bedrooms. We chose one with a big window open to the sea a few yards from the bed. We drew back the pink curtains, opened the window a crack, and the swish of fjord and roar of river filled the little bedroom. There is no such sleep, no such music to calm the interior frenzy, to lullaby your demons into drooling irrelevance. Someday you are going to die. So what? The human race is endlessly foolish. So what? You are broke and almost old. So what? God may or may not exist in some form. So what? It's up to him. Or her. Or neither. Or both. So what? Still light. Always light.

Someone once asked me about the size of the lots for the old houses at the bottom of the hill in Hofsós. Who knows? So what? These fifteen houses—Ás, Garður, Krossafell, Síða, Sæberg, Sólvík, Braut, Gilsbakki, Brattahlíð, Sólvangur, Brimnes, et al.—are a wonderful jumble, like a child's spilled Lego blocks. None are large, but none are the same size, shape, or color. Some are stuccoed, some timber covered with iron, one pure painted timber. All the roofs are multicolored: red, green, black, silver, gold, orange.

The oldest house—one of three closest to the sea, and hardly larger than a doll's house—is painted two shades of bright peach. The house is split vertically, shared by my neighbor Villi and a lady from Reykavjík who arrives occasionally. Both own one room up, one down, and half a cellar. An enthusiastic gardener, Villi has lined his half with plastic-covered flower boxes, tending them daily and lovingly, occasionally brushing June snow off the plastic, opening the tops to the sun as the day warms.

In Sæberg—a tiny, square, bright blue house that may, in fact, be three or four feet closer to the sea than Brimnes—lives my other neighbor, Hallgrímur. With a spade and a wheelbarrow, Hallgrímur dug out a basement beneath his one-room house. There he installed a huge bathtub facing a large window looking out to the fjord, saying, "It's fine to have a large tub where a man can lie in warm water with a good book and a glass of whiskey and watch the sea a few feet away." My neighbor Hallgrímur is a wise man.

By my third or fourth trip to Hofsós I had fallen completely in love with the place, so much so that it had become my imaginary sveit. I heard the tale of a filmmaker from the States who had coproduced a film with the local genius Friðrik Þór, in the process falling, like me, in love with the place. He had bought a concrete house up in the new "main" town. I bemoaned the poverty of poets when I found out he'd paid several million for the place. Only to learn not long after that those millions were krónur, not dollars, whereupon the price descended seventy- or eightyfold.

"Even I could afford that!" I babbled happily. "But I suppose there is nothing for sale."

I poured another Brennivín for myself and Valgeir, who pondered deeply, raised one eyebrow, and said, "I think Brimnes is the house for you." We were sitting in it, watching the pink and gold light on Tindastóll, the mountain just over the fjord. The window was open to sea slosh and the shrieking of terns fishing in the tide to feed their chicks.

"You wouldn't . . . ," I said.

"I would," he said, and named a figure. Without, as I remember, a further word, we shook hands, drained glasses, poured another to *skál*, and that, as the Icelanders say, was namely that.

Brimnes is a trailer-shaped rectangle facing the sea. It's still small, hardly eight hundred square feet, but it was once even smaller. Built of cheap lumber sometime in the twenties, the little house was originally two-thirds its present size, but when the sixth or seventh pregnancy was underway a previous owner added two more small bedrooms to the north end of the house. The original contained a shotgun kitchen with a trap door leading down to a low, dirt-floored basement filled with fishing gear. There was also a tiny bedroom facing south, a small sitting room, and another, slightly larger, bedroom. Water from a pump and no toilet—chamber pots only, probably emptied into the sea. The "new" wing from the thirties added, in addition to the two small bedrooms, a narrow entry hall and that blessed wonder, an indoor toilet.

Brimnes was never a rich man's house. The eighth pregnancy, as I heard the story, drove the family up the hill to bigger quarters, whereupon an old couple moved in. He died, she lived on and on. Finally the house stood empty, rotting back into the hillside, until Valgeir bought it and, with his brother Þórhallur, restored it to sturdiness and charm. Old photographs show it painted blue, but now it is sided and roofed with sheet iron to save it from the corrosive salting of the sea, and painted tan with a red roof, which nicely complements Villi's two-tone peach and Hallgrímur's dignified blue. Icelanders who endure long winter darkness and stretches of gray fog and drizzle fancy a certain efflorescent gaiety in their house colors. An old man just atop the hill painted his small concrete house in stripes of orange and lavender. It matched the sunset well. He's tamed it down recently to blue and white, but I miss that gypsy touch.

So I come here to this spare place in the summer, and sometimes in the winter when its spareness is magnified by snow and darkness. After a while, the United States is simply too much: too much religion and not enough gods, too much news and not enough wisdom, too many weapons of mass destruction—or, for that matter, of private destruction (why search so far away when they live right under our noses?), too much entertainment and not enough beauty, too much electricity and not enough light, too much lumber and not enough forests, too much real estate and not enough earth, too many books and not enough readers, too many runners and not enough strollers, too many freeways, too many cars, too many malls, too many prisons, too much security but not enough civility, too many humans but not enough eagles. And the worst excess of all: too many wars, too much misery and brutality—reflected as much in our own eyes as in those of our enemies. So I come here to this spare place. A little thinning and pruning is a good anodyne for the soul. We see more clearly when the noise is less, the objects fewer.

When Americans ask me to describe my little house in Iceland, I tell them, not entirely disingenuously, that it is a series of magical windows with a few simple boards to hold them up, to protect your head from rain while you stare out to sea. Though the sitting room is small, its two windows frame expansive views: one facing southwest toward the back of the fjord, with Mælifell (the "measuring mountain," highest in the fjord and crowned with a real cone peak) and the lights of the country town fifteen miles away across the water, and the other looking northwest past the fishing harbor along the whole length—thirteen miles—of Tindastóll, then to the lower sea cliffs north of it. I brag that I own the most romantic toilet on the planet. I do not joke; the view is the same as that from the sitting room. The partition between the two small north bedrooms came down, and one can now lie all night looking northwest to fjord, mountain, harbor, the north end of Hofsós with the old Danish pack house from the eighteenth century, and the pale green Emigration Center. And always, of course, the endless, kaleidoscopic summer light. The blinds are never drawn, the windows forever open a crack, whatever the temperature. (Iceland is never hot—65° is tropical, 45° or 50° usual, 60° ambrosial.) There are no screens—for no mosquitoes. In high summer, sleepy flies entertain me. I swat them with regret.

In the back of the house, the windows face a grassy meadow, the gravel street going steeply uphill, the world of neighbors, and, lowering over them, the mountains to the east. Here is the tiny spare room and the narrow kitchen where coffee is brewed and fish boiled. I've kept the stove and refrigerator, though both are at least fifty years old. They suit this modest workman's house. The Electrolux has a broken freezer door and must be continually defrosted. But then a little fresh ice, much less a little labor, never hurt a man. The freezer always holds a bottle of ice-sheathed Brennivín, the Icelandic schnapps used to bid guests welcome, and often a forgotten fish, its melancholy tail protruding from a miniature, artificial glacier. The made-in-Iceland Rapha stove (Marcy says it sounds like the name of a Hindu god, maybe of fire) is itself ancient, probably more than fifty years old. My age? Who knows? It is indestructible, and will surely outlast the house and me and you too. It is all spun steel—burners, frame, broiler—covered with white enamel porcelain. It has three burners, small, medium, and large—or, as they are named on the stove, *V* for *vinstri* (left), *A* for *aftur* (back), and *H* for *hægri* (right). They all work perfectly. The Rapha boils, fries, bakes, and grills dependably. It is a simple, sturdy machine designed to last—and to function. Those of you who are continually upgrading the machines of daily life at ever-greater expense and ever-increasing complexity ought to think long and hard on the old Rapha. Your new machine will improve neither the quality of your cooking skills nor the splendor of the ingredients. My fish will always be fresher and tastier than your fish, as will my lamb chops, and none of your money or machinery will ever alter that fundamental fact. We all need new ideas, images, and experiences far more than we need new stoves or cars or computers. The haddock swimming in the fjord a half hour ago is ready to go into the pot. The waxy yellow potatoes grown a few miles away are already boiling. There's plenty of local cream to whip for the arctic blueberries picked on the cliff next to Þórðarhöfði, and the happiest butter you have ever eaten is melting slowly in a banged-up saucepan. The wine will be French, South African, or Australian, and admittedly, a smidgeon overpriced, but we cannot demand perfection in an imperfect world.

Years ago I bought a small piano for the sitting room, a Yamaha far from home. Too small, to be sure, for Rachmaninoff, the *Hammerklavier,* or the big Liszt, but it is adequate for Scarlatti, Haydn, the homier Schumann, and, of course, Bach. There are no bad instruments for Bach, even if you have to play him on a cardboard box and imagine the music. Singers, cellists, flautists, and four-hand partners stop by regularly to provide musical company and entertainment. Valgeir's twelve-year-old daughter, Solveig, comes to practice her piano lesson and to investigate the chocolate supply. I am free of the television, computers, and the telephone in Brimnes, but I weakened a year ago and bought a cheap boom box, mostly to play Icelandic singers when guests come. All my Icelandic visitors have multiple cell phones that ring in chorus continually— "William Tell Overture" fights it out with "Loch Lomond," "Turkey in the Straw," Mozart's "Turkish Rondo," "Für Elise," and "Swan Lake," among others. If cell phones are necessary—a position I question—best to have these musical rings. I honor the habits of my guests in any case.

But what modern technical noises—for that matter, what music, even Bach—can compete with the music of water, river, and fjord, constantly in motion? To extend the metaphor, what artwork that you hang on your walls can stand up to the splendor of the light that enters this house? It is good that humans labor to make beauty out of light and sound and language, but we must also practice a certain modesty in the presence of our superior—the world out those windows.

SKAGAFJÖRÐUR

I grew up on the tallgrass prairie of the Midwest, looking out my windows not at lakes, rivers, or even sloughs, but rather at miles of corn and soybeans. The sluggish brown rivers dried up in August, the sloughs and ponds froze solid in November, and the numerous lakes were to the north and east. Yet throughout my boyhood, I dreamed of the sea—the pitch and roll of swells far from land. I read Dana's *Two Years Before the Mast*, Melville's and Conrad's sea novels, Walt Whitman's "Out of the Cradle Endlessly Rocking," Byron's apostrophe "Roll on, thou deep and dark blue Ocean...." I was not charmed by Laura Ingalls Wilder or even by Ole Rölvaag, except for his metaphor of an ocean of grass with the wakes from the prairie schooners opening through it. I wanted tides and rollers and above all immensity. To arrive at Brimnes in middle age was thus the fulfillment of a lifetime of longing delivered.

We do not see reality—or nature—directly, but always through a window of some sort. These windows are often physical, the window of our "place," our experience, our particular angle onto nature. But they can also be mental, the window of our prejudices, ignorance, ancestors, income, the boundaries we erect around the imagination. The events of our lives, both private and public, spiritual and political, enter the consciousness through these dirty, smudged, undersized windows. St. Paul says we see only "through a glass, darkly." Maybe the sea, so big, so deep, so beyond our power to order, so completely without opinions about what it swallows or what gifts it gives, can provide us with clearer views of our own lives, our country, our connection to others and to history. If, in addition, that sea is flooded with unending light for three months, we might more clearly apprehend whatever wisdom arrived through those windows. At any rate, I thought so as a boy, that the world would look clearer if there were a sea out the window, and now I have been given a chance to see whether that intuition will prove itself.

West of Brimnes lies the United States, my home, my citizenship, my burden, and probably most of my character, my prejudices, my opinions. What does it look like from here? I have passed sixty—not old these days, perhaps, but old enough to know that I am not eternal. What does this more-than-half century of my life look like? This is, of course, Henry Thoreau's question in *Walden*. Henry found his angle of vision at his cabin on Walden Pond. I had to go outside the United States to find mine. The country has gotten too big, too noisy, too populated, too frenzied—probably too brainlessly religious, media crazed, shopaholic, and warlike for me to see anything but a vast cloud of human white noise. So I found a little Walden cabin far away, very far away, in every possible sense of far—with a set of wonderful, huge windows facing west over the sea. What does that which I've loved—people, music, language, nature— amount to from these windows? These grand windows framed by a few simple boards become an instrument, a metaphor, an angle, a perspective from which to consider what has come of America.

Skagafjörður is the best-designed fjord in Iceland for geographical claustrophobes. Compared to the others I've seen in Norway, Scotland, Alaska, and British Columbia, I might award it planetary honors. It possesses all necessary ingredients of fjord-ness: saltwater, precipitous mountains, a scattering of handsome islands, cliffs, and headlands, all evidence of the hard work of glaciers for eons, and here in Iceland of the uprising of volcanoes. Its sixteen-mile-wide mouth opens straight north into what is probably no longer the North Atlantic but rather the Arctic Ocean. The Arctic Circle wends its invisible way around the globe's neck about forty miles north as the raven flies. In the summer, from late May until barely-August, the sun feigns setting not in the west but in the north, though it never really sets at all. It only grazes the surface of the sea for a moment, turning the sky orange, pink, lavender, and gold, then proceeds to pull itself up by its bootstraps to the top of the sky again. For a few hours the world is pale gray and pink, quite bright enough to read whatever newspaper you have acquired to distract yourself from the splendors of the spectacle. The sea often turns an intense pink shot through by gold stripes. If a man wore a suit colored like this to an office or a bank, no one would dream of doing business with him. But then I suppose the sun is a poor model for moving securities.

Some fjords have narrow dark mouths, puritans who dare you to enter their inner space, rock walls that eat an hour or two of light at either end of the day, leaving the sea and any towns or farms inside lit by flickering shadows. I do not prefer such places. Skagafjörður is a fat fjord with a wide mouth open to all the light it can drink, every last smidgeon it can suck out of the sun, or even an intense winter moon or the northern lights. This is not a Savonarola or Cotton Mather fjord but rather a laughing Buddha fjord, a Falstaff fjord, a fjord that embraces the visible world.

Do I anthropomorphize a fjord too much? Nonsense, I cannot anthropomorphize enough. If people have characters peculiarly their own, why should we deny one to a fjord? If we believe one place no different from another in its nature or its suitability to our own character, then we are so lost in cyberspace that we may as well be mice locked in a windowless box lit only by humming circuits and flickering dots on a screen. Your place on this planet, if you are a human of some sort, is where (among other things) the light feels right to you. The light in Skagafjörður feels right to me, and, with remarkable consistency, to other travelers intrepid enough to arrive here.

If you wish to observe the Icelandic landscape, you had best like the long view. There are plenty of lava caves and glacial crevasses to disappear inside, but other than the medieval outlaws, Icelanders have never preferred them. They build their homes and farms on rises, to see and to be seen. It helps the long view that Iceland is almost free of trees, as well as of all reptiles, amphibians, large predatory mammals, and almost all insects. Nothing large, hungry, dangerous, or numerous will interfere with your long view.

Most travelers arrive at Skagafjörður from the southwest of Iceland. This is the right first view, the right direction of approach. As in the first lovemaking, the first funeral, the first harbinger of your own mortality, this first view should be memorable. Here are directions.

Unless you are lucky enough to come by sea, you will land at an airport indistinguishable from those in Buffalo, Sioux Falls, Albuquerque, Toronto, or Cincinnati. Humans have finally invented a completely placeless place—hermetically sealed, security-inspected, dislocated boredom. Never mind. You are only four- or five-odd hours from where you want to be. When you step out of the airport, which occupies the end of the Reykjanes Peninsula, you will find yourself on a long lava outflow, almost without vegetation, rough, craggy, and bleak. Take heart. Just north of the thirty-mile highway to Reykjavík, the sea charges onto the lava, and, on a clear day,

Snæfellsjökull, a mile-high mountain crowned with a glacier, rises as if straight out of the sea seventy or eighty miles north. Reykjavík is now a real city, with suburbs, shopping malls, traffic jams, housing developments, billboards for the world's goods. You can visit its fleshpots later and even discover its many charms, but for now, point like a dog toward a doomed bird, turn north on Highway 1—the Icelandic national ring road—and drive straight out of town, keeping Esja, the local mountain, hard on your right, and the sea (here mostly tide flats) to your left. A few adventurous Icelanders have planted Alaskan blue spruce to clutter the landscape with trees. Ignore them. The Icelanders mean well, to soften their bare, wild landscape of grass and rock and ice, to make it more like other places, less harsh and grand. The Icelandic native tree, a gnarled dwarf birch seldom taller than a medium-sized Icelander, looks more at home—because it is, of course, at home. It inspired everybody's favorite Icelandic forest joke: What do you do if you find yourself lost in an Icelandic forest? Stand up.

Until a few years ago, drivers heading north enjoyed their first of Iceland's multitudinous fjords—Hvalfjörður, the Whale Fjord. But prosperity, engineering skill, and the desire to move from one place to another more quickly and uneventfully conspired to tunnel the mouth of the fjord. For a thousand krónur you disappear under the sea for four miles and emerge, having saved yourself the trouble of sixty miles of craggy mountains, at an old whale-cutting station, amongst the ghosts of British and American fortifications built to save Iceland from Hitler's clutches.

Pass through the town of Borgarnes, stopping, if hunger overwhelms you, at one of the four gas stations and convenience stores that sell the Icelandic hot dog—a mild lamb sausage slathered with pink remoulade sauce and a dollop of crisply fried onion bits. North of town, you leave the sea for a while and drive through valleys dotted with farms, summer-houses, lava outcrops, and multicolored buttes that will remind you a little of the landscape of old western movies. The land now rises fifteen hundred feet, the vegetation thins. You have climbed Holtavörðuheiði, a high, barren moor with a big mountain—the Troll's Church—rising to the west. Though you now drive on a fine, hard-surfaced two-lane road, and an electronic gizmo on the way up announces the temperature and road conditions on the pass, the old, potholed gravel road winds along parallel to you, just to remind you that until fifteen years ago driving over this heath was an adventure in motoring. In those days, the moor was said to be haunted, but the modern road seems to have banished any ghosts. Pity.

Holtavörðuheiði, though it is hardly fifteen hundred feet high, divides Icelandic weather from south to north as Caesar divided Gaul. If it is raining and blustery in Reykjavík and Borgarfjörður, the sun frequently appears to the north and east from the top of the moor. Just past the little orange shelter hut for stranded travelers at the top of the pass, the sea comes into view again, steeply below you, two small finger fjords ringed with low grassy hills—Hrútafjörður (the Ram's Fjord) and Miðfjörður (the Middle Fjord)—and, if you are lucky and the day clear, two glaciers to the east, Eiríks and Langjökull, and the craggy mountains of the "westfjords."

A curious feature of Icelandic weather is that the north usually has more sunny, clear days than Reykjavík in the southwest. The Gulf Stream, which flows close to the southwest coast, is a mixed blessing. Though it keeps Reykjavík temperate and often free of snow in the winter, it brings with it bouts of eternal rain, bad-tempered winds, and leaden skies. The warm current weakens before it reaches the north coast and drops most of its moisture on the interior glaciers, creating sometimes a version of an arctic Costa del Sol.

A couple of pleasant coffee shop truck stops await you at the bottom of the pass. This is the halfway point for traffic to Akureyri, the major town on the north coast. No Icelandic trip goes on for long without a little coffee and a little something else. *Kleinur*? *Kjötsúpa*? A little haddock hot dish—*plökkfisk*? A striped cake with rhubarb filling? And always, as the Icelanders say, ten more drops of coffee. From this point on, there are almost no trees at all.

Drive onward through Húnavatnssýsla County, one of the longer stretches of straight and uneventful road in Iceland. But be careful not to speed. The police in the county town, Blönduós (the mouth of the Blanda River), are famous both for their numbers (nine—almost an army in this thinly peopled country) and for their vigilance. Until the last fifteen years, Iceland had few hard-surfaced roads outside Reykjavík and the airport, but Icelanders drove ferociously on the potholed one-and-a-half-lane gravel. I couldn't imagine police in those days driving anything but four-wheel drive tow trucks to rescue cars or trucks lost up to their axles in sticky mud or vast washouts. But now, when it is theoretically possible to drive briskly on these almost-empty but nonetheless well kept roads, the Blönduós police will find and fine you if you have exceeded a stately 90 kilometers per hour. Any Icelander will present you with a long and entertaining saga: my traffic tickets in Húnavatnssýsla.

I have some experience myself. Four or five years ago, driving through Húnavatnssýsla for the first time in twenty years, I came over a small rise to see flashing police lights headed my way. I stopped, not imagining what offense I might have committed. I spoke English to the officer on the old principle: play dumb abroad. No use. He informed me briskly and in quite serviceable English that I had been radared at 110 kilometers and the speed limit was 90 kilometers, and that, thank you very much, would cost me seven thousand krónur (about a hundred dollars at the time). Furthermore, he said after a cursory glance at my Minnesota driver's license, I must pay him immediately and he would accept Visa. Visa? Visa, indeed. I handed him the credit card, which he examined with much greater care than he had the driver's license, whipped a portable gizmo out of his uniform pocket, swiped my card, handed the gizmo to me for signature, briskly tore off the receipt, wished me to "have a nice day," mounted his cruiser, and took off heading west, his radar tuned to nab the next malefactor.

A year or two later, the county police (*Lögreglan*—an unpronounceable word) added a new fillip. I'd gone to Hveravellir, a magical hot spring in a high desert oasis between two enormous glaciers deep in the interior of the country, but still in Húnavatn County. Icelandic country roads are full of sheep gates and, as shotgun rider in my friend Jón Magnússon's enormous Fjallabíl (a juiced-up remodeling of an old Ford Econoline), I was the appointed gate man. The green, steaming oasis, dotted with wildflowers among the smoking fumaroles, had just appeared, a wild mirage between walls of ice, after fifty-plus miles of bare, trackless gravel. I had opened the last gate and got into my seat for the last hundred and fifty yards of road when the county police appeared, lights flashing. Jón did not look pleased. He addressed them, of course, in proper Icelandic. "Surely we weren't speeding?"

"Your front-seat passenger is not wearing his seat belt, and that is, of course, a seven-thousand-krónur fine."

"But he just opened the gate less than a minute ago to go to Hveravellir a few yards away."

"That is no excuse for a violation of the seat belt regulation, of course, but we are feeling lenient today, so we shall issue you only a warning. Have a nice day." And with that the officer handed Jón a handsome group photo of the county police and rescue squad, nine strong, smiling sweetly: always on duty to protect you, if mostly from your own bad habits.

As you drive through Húnavatn County, fiddle with your radio. You travel in Hallbjörn Hjartarson country—*Íslensk Kantry tónlist*, Icelandic country western. Hallbjörn broadcasts from the second floor of his American-style saloon. Kantrybær is in the village of Skagaströnd, an old Viking trading post on the west side of the Skagi Peninsula. Hallbjörn, a balding, ponytailed curmudgeon in his sixties, has been singing and broadcasting cowboy music in this wild country for years. It goes well—broken hearts, loneliness on the road, faithful horses and faithless women, all with proper guitar slides and twangs. Mozart does not go well in this stern landscape. Too urbane. Too civilized, in the manner of old Europe. This is Europe, yes, but its fringe, its outrigger, its last trading post before the high arctic.

At this point, the almost-deserted Skagi Peninsula tempts the traveler to enter Skagafjörður from the back side on a properly rugged road. Skagi is a fat thumb (or phallus, if your mind works in that direction) of rock that forms the west coast of Skagafjörður. Your first view is of its wide mouth looking inland. Continue east on Highway 1 past Blönduós, where the Blanda River threads its way through a small gorge into the sea.

You drive now through the long, narrow valley—aptly called *Langidalur*—that follows the handsome Blanda River. The river is chockablock with fat salmon, and in season you can watch many a pair of hipboots trying their luck, flycasting (for a fee fat as the salmon) in high hopes. In summer the boggy ditches next to the river fill with a tone poem of arctic wildflowers: violets, cotton grass, buttercups, marsh marigolds, pink, lavender, gold, white. The farms here look prosperous and the sheep fat, contented, and a little stupid.

You have left the sea for a while now, but have faith. It sloshes dependably just to the north of these mountains. You begin climbing a long rise out of Langidalur, perhaps a thousand feet to the Vatnsskarð pass. A few small lakes decorate the Vatnsskarð pass, but fishing is probably cheap here—only pink trout. The yellow poles along the road that guide the snowplow driver grow taller and taller as you rise. At sea level they are only a few feet high, but here they rise above your car roof. Usually, on this small pass, the light begins to intensify, to acquire that clarity and immensity of true Skagafjörður light. You are close now.

Slow down as you begin to descend. The bottom is about to drop out of your view of the world. I do not exaggerate. Even a garrulous old fool cannot exaggerate an experience such as this.

At Arnarstapi, partway down the hill, the Icelanders have erected a memorial cairn—with bronze plaque of a mustachioed head and a few lines of verse—to their greatest emigrant poet. Stephan G. Stephansson, born on a farm near here in 1853, left the fjord in 1873, and died on a farm in Alberta facing the Rockies in 1927. He created one of the great bodies of work in the Icelandic language in the twentieth century, including a long poem attacking World War I and the human weakness for military violence, which almost got him jailed in Canada. Because he chose to write in Icelandic rather than English, almost no one in North America can read him now, but the Icelanders—particularly the Skagfirðingur, his old neighbors and relatives—read him passionately. Icelanders decorate the whole countryside with monuments to their literary history. Poetry is their glory and their internal cement as human beings, and they mean to remind you, the foreign traveler, as well as each other, of that central fact.

There's a little gravel pull-off next to the cairn. Stop. Get out of your car. Look. In any direction at all. Hope for a clear, bright day—it increases the distance and size of what you see—but remember, there is no bad weather in which to see Skagafjörður for the first time. If the whole fjord is buried in gray sea fog, as often happens, it will undoubtedly be a fog of great eeriness and mystery. The universe still has surprises in store for you—often when you least expect them.

Here, below this small hill, lies all of Skagafjörður, a wide body of water opening forty miles to the north. The islands: Drangey halfway up the fjord, a sheer-sided lump of round rock, six hundred feet high; to the north and east the huge, broken cliff of Þórðarhöfði, from here an apparent island but in fact connected to the mainland by a frail and narrow isthmus; and beyond that Málmey, looking like a sleeping giant laid out on the sea. To the west, Tindastoll, a thirteen-mile-long slab of mountain, and beneath it the county town Sauðárkrókur (Sheep River Hook), where a mountain stream curves abruptly to enter the fjord. To the east the snowy crags of Tröllaskagi, the highest and most rugged mountains in north Iceland, valley after deep valley opening between them, each backed by a small glacier that feeds the west-running rivers. South is Mælifell, a perfect cone mountain, highest in the fjord. Below you, the braided glacial-outwash river Héraðsvötn spreads out over a wide channel filled with green water meadows— perhaps fifty farms in view, the hay fields decorated with thousands of round, white plastic-wrapped bales. Swivel a bit, as if you were a human lazy Susan: you can see thirty or forty miles in all directions. This is the long view. This is Skagafjörður. There will be no claustrophobia here, only an immensity of air, light, water, sky, mountain, and glacier, all populated by handsomely placed farms, rich grass, sheep, horses, cows, and a few thousand fortunate Icelanders. All you need now is a few lines of properly rhymed Icelandic poetry to mumble to yourself as you begin simultaneously weeping and laughing.

I've learned to be dignified, even civilized, when others are present for this view at Arnarstapi. But when I come alone, I cannot help myself. I burst into tears and blubber like a fool. Sheer joy! Between blubbers, I begin laughing uproariously. What a world! What a universe! What a pleasure to be alive and sentient at such a place, on such a day. I could say—with my old Dakota neighbors from Minnesota—it is a good day to die. Which means, of course, that it is a good day to be completely alive, and particularly so when I look upon my humble abode, which has just now come into view where the Hof River runs down out of the mountains to join the fjord. A claustrophobe's dream—that vastness and light exist out all my windows. Finally, I am home.

ETHEREAL FRIENDS

Iceland is a spare place. When humans arrived here in the ninth century, they found a complete fauna of one terrestrial animal: the arctic fox. Small, shy creatures, they were not native to the island, but had likely arrived on ice that wandered east from Greenland. The sea had washed carrion up onto the beaches, the rivers were full of fish, and millions of birds nested in meadows and on cliffs. The fox found food and lodging, so they stayed, bred, and prospered. They had the island to themselves, no predators to make their lives dangerous—with the possible exception of an occasional eagle or gyrfalcon. Only the uncertainties of weather and dinner limited their numbers, but like the Icelanders themselves, they were never numerous. Nature provided them with a small niche, and they filled it modestly. Their reputation for slyness to the contrary, they seem by nature to be mostly reserved and private creatures, contented solitaries.

I suppose that I have now spent, of my sixty-odd years, five in Iceland during all seasons, yet I have never seen a fox. I often ask Icelanders if they've met one, but only perhaps half respond affirmatively. The whole native terrestrial fauna is, if nothing else, discreet. The settlers arrived with horses, cattle, sheep, dogs, and cats; ships brought rats and mice; and optimistic entrepreneurs brought mink and reindeer, both of whom proved to be business failures but nonetheless managed to escape and survive. The now-wild reindeer, delicious and much prized, graze in otherwise uninhabitable highlands, but the mink (here as elsewhere) are unloved and unwanted neighbors to humans, livestock, and birds. The Icelanders consider the shooting of mink—or, for that matter, of fox—a valuable national service. Despite so few animals in their list of fauna, they prefer still fewer. They await the extinction of both mink and rat with joy. The mice, on the other hand, provide amusement and nourishment for the army of Icelandic cats and the occasional bird of prey.

In the last thousand years, a handful of polar bears have arrived—traveling, like the fox, on ice—as unwanted guests from Greenland. Since there's nothing here for them to eat except Icelanders and valuable domestic animals, the Icelanders shoot them promptly. No one wants their sleep troubled by large predators in need of a meal. The modern Icelander who has not left the island has thus never seen a reptile, nor an amphibian, nor skunk, coyote, muskrat, raccoon, rabbit, gopher, beaver, wolf, bear, cougar, nor any large ungulate like elk, moose, or bison.

Neither has the Icelander been tortured by mosquitoes, biting blackflies, horseflies, nor any of that army of insect pests that bring disease, misery, and annoyance to most of the rest of us. It is the only mosquito-free zone in the far north; Greenland, Canada, Alaska, Siberia, and Scandinavia all require repellent poison, face nets, and forbearance. To experience Arctic light and landscape without slapping, scratching, slathering, or cursing, you must be in Iceland. And I, for one, am happy to be here.

There are no screens on the windows of any house in Iceland—at least none that I have visited. But the birds must have something to eat. Fortunately for them, a nice crop of flies (buzzers, not biters) comes to life on any sunny day in summer. They include a few fat and spirited bluebottles, but most are ordinary houseflies. During a long warm spell a few

summers ago, I wearied of them and went off to a local store in
search of a fly swatter. I tried to explain to the puzzled clerks
in my appalling Icelandic just what I was looking for—a little
plastic gadget to slay flies. Sometimes the response was the
classic, "Hah?" ("What the hell are you trying to say? I can't
understand a word of it . . ."). And sometimes, "Just use newspaper. Or simply be patient and ignore them. They'll go away
eventually." Like Pangloss, I inquired everywhere, boring all the
neighbors almost beyond endurance, but in the end I couldn't
even find an Icelandic word for fly swatter. I was complaining
to her uncle one day when Vala—a fourteen-year-old intellectual in training—looked up over the tops of her glasses from
the book she was reading and said, "*Flugnaspaði.*" Literally,
"fly spade." She resumed with her book.

"Good god!" I said. "That can't be it!"

"That's it," she said calmly. "Only you won't be able to find
one around here. Probably not even in Reykjavík."

She was right. Before my next trip to Iceland, I brought a
half dozen (79¢ apiece) from a hardware store in the States.
I was a popular fellow for a season or so, but one phlegmatic
Icelander remarked that the morning paper worked just as well,
was probably cheaper, and provided the additional pleasure of
seeing politicians' faces bespattered with smashed fly guts.

A few moths, a tiny red spider, a long-legged water strider,
some no-see-ums, a few more unidentified creatures—and with
that you've exhausted the extent of insect life in most of Iceland,
with two exceptions. The two largest lakes, Þingvallavatn and
Mývatn, are afflicted by swarming, biting midges—the *mý* in
the name of the lake—for a month or two each summer. Both
lakes are famous and popular tourist destinations, but I leave
them to the tourists, preferring to be reminded of their beauties
by eating the sweet, fat trout harvested from them. And then
in the spring a rich crop of bumblebees keeps busy fertilizing

the local flowers. These bees are particularly mammoth, the size of big, hairy marbles with motors buzzing inside. They terrify the Icelanders, who endure with great stoicism volcanic eruptions, quicksand, blizzards, and avalanches, but fear stingers. I've seen a room in an Akureyri restaurant vacated in a flash by the noisy presence of one bee in a window, until a brave customer singlehandedly murdered the bee. Only then did the slightly shaken patrons resume dining. We all fear surprises, the unusual, but are hardly troubled by those normal, everyday terrors.

But if the earth here is sparely inhabited by human, animal, tree, or crop, the air above it is filled with a veritable multitude of wings and feathers and songs. Indeed, Iceland, particularly in spring and summer, is a birder's Valhalla. It is impossible even for a thickheaded bookworm like me to ignore the presence of birds, though for a long time I made the pretense of doing so. "Birds interest me only when they are turning golden in a roasting pan. I am more curious about the sauce than about the identity of the bird." So said my inner idiot. But the continued presence of birds finally charmed me and roused my curiosity. At almost sixty, I began to understand the madness of my American friends who compiled "life lists," bought bags of suet and seed, rose at dawn for the annual bird counts, kept their binoculars and Peterson's guides always close at hand, rolled slowly down gravel roads with their heads hanging out the window, and visited sloughs without shotguns. Given a longer life, I might have turned into one of them, but I will probably always remain a peripheral birder, like a lover of string quartets who doesn't know a violin from a viola. Birding, like music, is an art that requires long practice, full attention, and a mysterious sixth sense of what goes on just outside the corner of the eye. It is a means of loving and respecting the natural world,

Nature with a capital *N*, as the eighteenth century had it. It is a form of meditation, and at its most profound a path to wisdom. But I remain, too, an unapologetic lover of the bird in the pan, the skin of a goose turning golden and crisp as it drops its fat, a pheasant taking its final bath in cream and wine, and, in Iceland, a dark breast of ptarmigan or puffin nestled beside a pot of wild berries on a white plate. The uses of nature are various and wonderful, and we are too shortly alive on earth to practice judgmental moralism. I, for one, am happy to look, to praise, to wonder—and sometimes to take and eat.

I suppose birds first entered my consciousness here through the windows. My little house faces a harbor where salt- and freshwater do combat twice a day. This roiling of waters must make a rich larder for sea birds and waders, since a half-dozen tribes of them are continually—and noisily—present from beginning to end of summer. This loud swarming of wheeling wings plays in the window frame like video outtakes from Hitchcock's *The Birds* or the splendid French documentary *Winged Migration*— much of it filmed not far away in north Iceland.

The peacekeepers in this lively gang of scavengers and hunters are the colony of eider ducks who nest nearby but come every day to dine in the tide. They satisfy the most rigorous American moralist by practicing sound "family values." Eiders clearly form pairs for breeding, Papa drake elegantly colored with black wings, a white breast, pink accents, and a sporty black cap on his head, Mama duck wearing a plain brown Harris-Tweed pattern—nothing flashy or untoward, both circling their pair of dull-colored, fuzzy chicks. As the season advances, Mama gives diving lessons to the chicks, first demonstrating the techniques, then leading them in the nose-down, arse-over-and-up dive. The chicks flounder awkwardly, seem almost to drown and come up empty-beaked, but presumably, like human children, they are capable of learning with practice. Eiders coo and gurgle and chortle quietly to each other, making true squawks only when startled or threatened. For a thousand years, Icelanders have gathered the down from these ducks. Until the twentieth century, every Icelander slept under an eider quilt—a *dúnsæng*—and many who can afford it still do. Like anything collected by hand from live creatures, eiderdown is now dear in every sense of the word. I've slept under a dúnsæng in Reykjavík, though I didn't like it. In spite of the fact that the down is almost weightless, they heat so efficiently that you wake in the middle of the night streaming with sweat, throw off the *sæng* with your feet, then wake half-frozen in ten minutes. Many Icelanders share my taste for sleeping in cold rooms with open windows, but in my experience the Icelandic climate is not quite savagely cold enough for the insulating power of eiderdown. It might come in handier in January in Minnesota, which has a true arctic climate despite being mostly at the latitude of Italy. The eider ducks, needless to say, do not migrate south for the winter. The Icelandic climate doesn't bother them at all. The sea here does not freeze.

The eiders are low flyers, awkward on takeoff but speedy in a straight line just above the surface of the sea. Soaring above them with a great noise, a couple of hundred arctic terns screech and cackle *fortissimo* as they swoop and dive into the sea for fish. They seldom miss. With a graceful plunge one strikes the waters, emerging with a small fish clenched triumphantly in its bright red beak. The trapped fish droops. As the tern rises, it shrieks raucously to celebrate its triumph in the hunt. The Icelandic name for the terns, *Kría!,* is wonderfully onomatopoeic—that is, it imitates the noise of the tern itself, and particularly when pronounced with an exclamation point.

The kría nest in large numbers along the gravel road just north of Hofsós. They protect their eggs and afterward their chicks with great ferocity, dive-bombing any human silly enough to walk through their territory. They have been known to draw blood by stabbing the heads of intruders with their sharp little beaks. Pugnacious devils they are, and the Icelanders treasure them for it. They are a small, elegantly designed bird, with red beak, pink feet, a black skullcap, a white breast, then bluish gray back feathers ending in a sharply forked tail.

The kría is the champion migrator, the highest-mileage flier among birds. They summer and breed in Iceland and much farther north, beyond the Arctic Circle in north Greenland, arctic Canada, Siberia; then in mid-August, just as the first dark arrives, they fly south, fishing for sustenance along the way, to winter in Tierra del Fuego or even the Antarctic, a round trip of some twenty-five thousand miles. And when they arrive back at the little lake in the middle of Reykjavík, they serve as the Icelanders' harbingers of spring. What spirit and energy in that tiny bird heart and brain! They must spend a greater part of their lives in pure, continuous light than any other creature. If god is light, then the kría—not man—is lord of creation. We could do worse for a metaphor, and usually have.

Fulmars—a full squadron!—and three or four kinds and sizes of gulls, black headed, black backed, herring, and common, join the commotion with the kría. An occasional raven flies over, adding his harsh croak, waiting for dinner scraps to clean up. The raven with its famously ugly voice is oddly enough classified in bird books as a "passerine," a songbird. The raven' a cousin of the meadowlark, the robin, the pipit, the warbler, and the mourning dove? Don't you have odd relatives yourself? Are you sure you look like your father?

In 2000, the Canadian writer David Arnason and I started a pair of early-summer Writer's Weeks, inviting participants to come to Hofsós for a week in either May or early June to write, talk about literature and ideas, and discover and enjoy Iceland. Many of the writers drawn to our Writer's Weeks were avid birders as well, tempted by the chance to see Icelandic birds during this optimal season when they settle in for the summer to breed and raise their chicks. For the first couple of years, David's friend John Weir came from Winnipeg to lead the birders out on expeditions. John is as passionate a birder as I've ever met and has written several lively books on his birding adventures. His own particular obsession in Iceland was to see the mysterious pink-footed goose. He found many, thus detracting from their mystery. But he also found, as all birders do, a cornucopia of waders—the long-billed, long-necked, long-legged stabbers into bogs, ponds, marshes, wetlands, and meadows close to the sea. Most winter farther south but prefer the far north for dining and breeding in the summer. Like humans, they are probably charmed by the long light. Watching John escort the workshop birders began to charm me as well. I soon found myself driving one kilometer per hour on the gravel road north of town, with the sea on the west and boggy meadows on the east, a perfect habitat for waders. My windows were open, my head frequently stuck out, my bird guide close at hand. I, too, had been bitten by the pleasures of birds.

Who wouldn't be charmed by these eccentric-looking—and often beautiful—samples of design in nature? I first discovered these birds in Icelandic, then had to memorize the English names. Here's a bilingual list of the common waders in this neighborhood:

Tjaldur — Oystercatcher
Jaðrakan — Black-tailed Godwit
Spói — Whimbrel
Heiðlóa — Golden Plover
Sandlóa — Ringed Plover
Hrossagaukur — Snipe

Stelkur — Redshank
Óðinshæne — Phalarope

These are not "tweetie" birds. In fact, with the exception
of whimbrel and plover, their voices are harsh and repetitive.
They sound like scolds, not opera stars. Their beaks are extraordinary; they are the Pinocchios of the bird kingdom. In the
case of the snipe, the beak is bigger than the bird. They dig and
poke in the bog mud, unearthing worms, minnows, insects, and
other wet creatures of slime and darkness. And they prosper.
Indeed, Hofsós, with its scant two hundred humans, is overwhelmed each summer by thousands of these winged and noisy
neighbors. They are my constant companions from mid-May
until—like me—they begin to pack and leave in mid-August.

Of all their ethereal friends, I think the Icelanders prefer
the plover and the whimbrel. The golden plover is a statuesque
and lovely bird, with its black breast and alert head. Its song
consists of a plaintive cooing, not unlike the sound of its own
name: *lóa*. The whimbrel, on the other hand, is colored in a dull
brown pattern, good for camouflage in an Icelandic meadow
but not the bird kingdom's most elegant suit of feathers. It is
loved above all for its long, warbling trill—and for its magnificent beak that curves sharply down at the end, looking always
as if it were about to scold you for unseemly behavior, such as
disturbing its nest during breeding and hatching season. That
beak has the look of wanting the last word in a conversation,
the last snap of wisdom.

The songs of these birds have generated thousands of lines
of Icelandic poetry. The symbols first of arriving spring and
then of the brief loveliness of an Arctic summer meadow, they
prompt the average Icelander to paroxysms of nostalgia and
nature mysticism. The birds become voices for the soul.

But my unsubtle eye prefers the oystercatcher and the black-
tailed godwit. These two, aside from sharing loud, monotonous,

repetitive songs—the oystercatcher's a single harsh "thweep" and the godwit's a crabby-sounding two-stroke that sounds like sticks banged together, "ack-ack"—share the peculiarity of being more beautiful in flight than in repose. The oystercatcher's eye, beak, and feet, in shades of bright pink, orange, and red respectively, could dance in a gypsy ballet without comment. But it is a sizable bird and when it opens its capacious wings to fly reveals a white belly, a symmetrical white stripe running down its almost-three-foot wingspan, finished with a rounded black tail. What a bold designer the natural selector proves itself to be!

The godwit is even more schizophrenic in design—two completely different birds at rest and in flight. I wrote this little prose poem shortly after making their acquaintance.

Black-tailed Godwit—Jaðrakan

He's walking on the gravel road north of town, an old fellow in a dusty auburn tailcoat with a bill as long and skinny as his neck or his toothpick legs. When I come too close, he opens his wings, leaves the earth for a hundred feet. As he flies overhead, I see what he's hiding—the flasher! He's wearing a ballroom floor in brilliant black and white, a modern painting fit to hang in the presidential suite! Such beauty you hide sitting on your post, you old fakir! He snaps his pointy tweezer beak, makes a harsh, loud two-note noise. "Keep my secret quiet, you nitwit," scolds Mr. Godwit as he settles his wings down atop a fence post to resume his lean, ascetic dignity. I won't divulge your secret beauty, I assure him, lying as usual.

Is this too anthropomorphic a bird for you? Do we—humans, poets, romantics, birders—project too much of our interior life into the tiny brain of a creature that is almost certainly pure instinct and no intellect? Well, so be it—or, to quote the Icelanders again, *"Það er nefnilega það"*—"that is certainly that."

Icelandic poetry probably exceeds English, even by sheer number of lines, in the anthropomorphizing of birds. With the possible exception of the Native Americans of the Pacific Northwest, the Icelanders are certainly the champion raven poets in any language or culture. In fact, the chief of the gods, Odin, is scarcely imaginable without his feathered friends. Here is Snorri Sturluson's description of him from *The Prose Edda*, translated by Jean Young:

> Two ravens sit on his shoulders and bring
> to his ears all the news that they see or hear;
> they are called Hugin (Thought) and Munin
> (Memory). He sends them out at daybreak to fly
> over the whole world, and they come back at
> breakfast-time; by this means he comes to know
> a great deal about what is going on, and on
> account of this men call him the god-of-ravens.
> As it is said:

> Over the world
> every day
> fly Hugin and Munin;
> I fear that Hugin
> will not come back,
> though I'm more concerned about Munin.

When the ravens are not busy spying for Odin, they join the wolf and eagle to do post-battle cleanup among the corpses. Though the raven is an ancient cliché—a formulaic pattern—in all old Teutonic poetry, the human race doesn't seem to have outgrown its need for this particular raven-work:

> *. . . the swept harp*
> *won't waken warriors, but the raven winging*
> *darkly over the doomed will have news,*
> *tidings for the eagle of how he hoked and ate,*
> *how the wolf and he made short work of the dead.*
>
> Beowulf, (Heaney, Seamus,
> translator, lines 3023–3027)

The Icelanders have further cause to be grateful to the raven, since the birds seem to have helped discover the island. Hrafna-Flóki Vilgerðarson (Raven-Floki) sailed west from Norway around 860, with three ravens aboard ship. He released the ravens one at a time. The first two returned, but he followed the lead of the third into Vatnsfjörð (Water Fjord) on the south side of the northwestern fjords. There he built a hut and spent the winter. The ruins of his hut are still clearly visible at Flókalundur, the oldest evidence of human habitation in Iceland. Old Hrafna-Flóki must have gotten bored at the end of a long, dark winter, so he climbed the nearby mountain Lónfell to have a peek into the next fjord. He looked down on floating icebergs, so he named his new and unpromising landfall "Iceland," and returned to Norway with the bad news. Flóki did return to Iceland, so we can assume, despite the icebergs, that he must have been charmed. But the name has stuck, and Icelanders have a raven to either praise or blame for it. They might have steered old Flóki toward Florida instead.

In both literature and music, the raven seems to have two opposite faces, melancholy and humor—maybe memory and thought? The melancholy is obvious: ravens are big and black everywhere, they sing in a harsh and ugly croak, and they dine wherever death has provided dinner for them. Yet there is also something jolly and friendly about ravens. They like people, keep them company, prance comically on their strong feet, and even entertain with musical airshows, the Charlie Chaplins of ornithology. Poe got the raven's voice entirely wrong, probably because he was more in love with the long *O* vowel than with verisimilitude. Ravens do not sing "nevermore"; they sing "krak," pronounced as "crock" with a trilled *R*. The Icelanders have clearly listened more closely.

The Icelanders have affectionate, often humorous nicknames for both humans and other creatures. They call the raven *Krummi*, which has a chummy ring. I've met several Krummis, including one of our local carpenters and handymen. There seems to be nothing melancholy or ominous about this wryly funny man, but he is, like his namesake bird, a good dancer, though probably not much of a singer.

Davíð Stefánsson, one of his country's best-loved poets, wrote perhaps the most famous raven poem in Icelandic. It paints a picture of a poor Krummi who wants only to sing a beautiful song, to be loved like other birds for his voice, but who is cursed with his ugly "krak." *Krummi* is an Icelandic nickname for the raven. Used without an accompanying swear-word, it has a certain connotation of fondness. It's a grand poem, often sung to a sad and lovely tune by Tryggvi Baldvinsson.

Krummi

Old Raven is black,
but Raven is my bird.
He croaks his songs
to the sky and the sun.
Krunk, krunk, krá.
Don't scorn the songs
that come from black breasts.

His heart, too, beats with love for the sun
though he wears black feathers—
black feathers even in sunlight.
Krunk, krunk, krá.
Some are under a spell
that allows no lovely tunes
though they yearn for nothing
more than for singing,
flying like the swan and singing.
Krunk, krunk, krá.
Raven owns no lovely notes.
Will never make a lovely sound.
Under his black cowl condemned to croak
'til his raven heart is broken—
his raven heart broken with yearning.
Old Raven is black,
but Raven is my bird.
He croaks his songs
to the sky and the sun.

Krummi provides a rich horde for metaphor, most of which probably irritates true birders, who like their facts straight and their bird talk unadorned by whimsy. But they must forgive the tribe of poets; the raven is simply irresistible. I went a few years ago to visit a finely restored old hotel, Tindastóll, in the neighboring town of Sauðárkrókur. Svanfríður and her husband, Pétur, saved the 1884 timber house from collapse, decorated and repaired it with great elegance, painted it in the old colors, and furnished it throughout with Icelandic antiques or good reproductions. They built—by hand—a stone-lined hot-spring bath and pool in the backyard, where they also kept a cage for Svanfríður's pet ravens. Their names? You guessed it. I looked at those caged ravens a long time, then wrote this description of the afternoon:

Ravens at the Hotel Tindastóll

In the garden behind the old hotel
Svanfríður shows me two ravens in a pen.
"Of course their names are Hugin and Munin."
Thought and memory. What else
would you call a pair of trapped ravens?
First the facts. They are black.
She says they are hardly more than chicks.
Dense foot-long body, a yard of wingspan,
a three-inch pincer beak that probably
could clip off your pinkie finger as if
it were Odin's other eye and fly away with it.
Their voice—a harsh, nasal rasp.
No nonsense about "nevermore."
"O" is not a raven vowel. He likes "aaaaa."
Trapped in this ten-foot raven prison,
Hugin and Munin have hardly room
to unfold and flap their jagged wings.
The look in their black eye is not happy,
but neither is it tamed and beaten.
No cowering in this pair.
They are not neat eaters, grass
littered with scattered scraps.
And how they can shit! Tan turds
the size of fat salamis everywhere.
I'd call them not thought and memory,
but power and cunning—the same quality
but the right name. No one loves
and protects the raven. He takes care of himself.
He does not need an agency
or program. Would not prefer to live
in a sanctuary. The world is his zone.
Wherever there is death, there is meat.

His motto is: take and eat.
When Jesus comes again in glory to judge
the quick and the dead, he had better
borrow this pair from Odin and wear them
on his white-robed shoulders to tell him
who's been up to what for good or ill
for a thousand generations now.
Whenever any gods arrive
how shall we know them
but by their ravens?
Only by their ravens.

If the raven excites melancholy in the breast of Icelanders, the ptarmigan sinks them into nostalgia, memories of Christmas Eve, childhood, mother's hands reaching into an oven, candles, old carols, a chaos of crumpled wrapping paper that once housed gifts, tales of the *Jólasveinar*—the Christmas trolls. For the *rjúpa*—Icelandic for the ptarmigan—is the Christmas-dinner bird. He arrives at table accompanied by sugared potatoes, *ora baunir* (canned, reconstituted dried peas—an Icelandic delicacy), red cabbage, a bowl of creamy gravy, and a pot of wildberry sauce. *Gleðileg jól*, my ptarmigan!

The cousin to pheasant, partridge, grouse, and woodcock, it is Iceland's only real ground-dwelling game bird, hunted in season usually from mid-October until a few days before Christmas. My neighbor ptarmigans nest and dine in tussocky meadows lining the gravel road north of town. In summer and autumn, their feathers are a dull gray brown, a nice match for the dry grass. As a summer resident, I generally see them with this unassuming plumage, though their peculiar genius is to molt three times a year. In winter, the male turns pure white, wearing a bright red comb above his eye—like lurid makeup! In spring, when they breed, they molt again, becoming pale brown with yellow flecks until they darken in the midsummer molt. If ptarmigans were human, we might accuse them of vanity, changing their plumage so often, but humans are not the only creatures to have discovered the pleasures of dining on the ptarmigans' plump breasts. The gyrfalcons fancy them too, and when the ptarmigans are a little late in their molt they become too visible to survive easily. This year, travelers on the Bær road frequently found piles of feathers attached to a beak, the tidy remnants of a falcon's dinner. But when the ptarmigan is in full camouflage, you become aware of them only when your approach flushes them out. Like their cousins the pheasant and partridge, they rise suddenly into the air with a great whirring of wings and a loud, alarmed belching. But don't reach for your shotgun for a few years yet. Unfortunately, the rjúpa is not the most brilliant of birds, and more than one Icelandic hunter has assured me that in fact you could probably bag your limit with a gunnysack and a baseball bat. The numbers of ptarmigan fluctuate wildly, from fifty thousand to two hundred thousand breeding pairs over a ten-year cycle. The numbers reached a low in 2003, whereupon the official custodians of nature in Iceland put a moratorium on the hunting season for three years. My generous friend Margret, on hearing that I hadn't eaten a rjúpa for twenty years, flushed the last dozen of them out of her freezer that July and cooked me a proper Christmas dinner in midsummer. The rjúpa were as delicious as I remembered them, though when the three-year hunting ban was announced in August, Margret sighed sadly; had she known of this, she might not have parted with her last rjúpa. I hardly blamed her, though I remained no less grateful for the grand feast.

Fortunately, the rjúpa seem to be recovering now, at least locally. I hardly travel the Bær road without scaring up at least a half dozen of them. Indeed, after breeding season I often have to slow down to one kilometer an hour, or even stop the car on the gravel road and wait ten minutes while a clucking rjúpa hen leads her six chicks in stately procession down the middle of the road. I think it's a mark of sanity and civilization to have all your errands postponed and your appointments canceled at the whim of a ptarmigan. Sit back and enjoy. Those chicks you saved will certainly grow up to adorn someone's Christmas table and bring joy on Christmas Eve. Skál to the rjúpa! May their numbers increase—and soon!

Aside from the resurrected ghost of the last great auk, eaten by Icelandic sailors in 1844 at Eldey, a sheer rock rising from the Atlantic off the southwest coast, birders come to Iceland to see the Big Three: gyrfalcon, white-tailed eagle, and gannet. All are large, powerful hunting birds, striking in flight or perching on their cliffs. Humans admire size in nature, preferably grappled to a frisson of fear. We prefer the polar bear or the grizzly, the anaconda or the cobra, the lion or the wolf to their smaller, friendlier brethren—the dog, the garter snake, the gecko, the box turtle, the house cat, or the Holstein. We like danger, predators who regard us as game rather than as master. But of these three, only the gyrfalcon is a true hunter. The eagle can use its great size to overmaster prey but, like the raven, generally prefers its dinner dead, even a little ripe. The gannet, so magnificent in the hunt, is a danger only to fish, but a great pleasure to watch for its lightning dives and deadly accuracy. It makes one grateful not to be a herring.

The birders who come to Hofsós usually long to see the falcon, the national bird and symbol of Iceland. Icelandic falcons are legendary. They have been prized as hunting birds since the Middle Ages and were for centuries a lucrative export all over the known world. Ottoman pashas, German barons, and Danish kings all hunted with this ferocious-eyed and taloned bird. But like any large predator, feathered or otherwise, falcons were never numerous. They require too large an area for their hunts and are not sociable birds. Many falcon pairs nest in the trackless jumble of lava around Mývatn, Midge Lake, in north Iceland. Haukur, the late husband of my cousin Cathy in Vopnafjörður, was once hired to patrol the lava, protecting the nests from poachers who tried to make off with the eggs and chicks. Why? I asked. "They sell them at a huge price to Arab oil sheikhs who fancy them for hunting. But the falcons cannot bear the great heat of the desert and soon die. Then the sheikhs buy more." What an odd fate, for an Arctic hunter to expire in the baking sand so far from his snow-swept eyrie.

One sunny afternoon a few years ago, the birders borrowed my car and drove south with John Weir as their guide. They drove deep into the mountains far south of Skagafjörður in hopes of seeing pink-footed geese. They were successful, and also spotted a number of other local birds on the way. Tired and delighted, they were returning to Hofsós when they stopped by the marshes at the bottom of the fjord to admire a peaceful family of eider ducks swimming in a salt pond: duck, drake, and two furry chicks, a happy eider family. Suddenly, as if from the cloud above, great wings descended with a whoosh, snatched up one of the eider chicks, and disappeared back into the cloud, all of it at lightning speed. The duck and drake growled and gawked, clearly upset. The birders, on the other hand, were ecstatic. My god, what luck! A falcon, so close! Another notch on the life list! They had almost finished congratulating themselves when the sky opened again—another rush of wings, the second and last chick trapped in talons, disappearing back into the air forever. The duck and drake cooed inconsolably—suddenly chick-less, a ruined family. But the birders could hardly believe their luck—two falcons at close range. The old cliché, that they saw "nature red in tooth and

claw," did not occur to them, nor should it have. Of course
nature has teeth. Everything eats everything else. It's a good
system generally. Only humans fail to eat what we kill. Only
humans kill abstractly, with projects, machines, poisons, and
schemes. We are right to admire the falcons for their power
and skill. Ólafur Nielsen, an Icelandic falcon researcher, reports finding these food remains near a single eyrie: two
whimbrels, three puffins, one snipe, two widgeons, two mal-
lards, seven arctic terns, and twenty-seven ptarmigan. The falcon, like the Icelander, seems to prefer the juicy ptarmigan as
a main course, but is perfectly happy to have an eider chick or
two as an appetizer. *Bon appétit*, Sir Falcon!

The pursuit of birds, aside from being an end in itself, provides an excuse for travel—often to wild, difficult, and beautiful places. The birds we find give us keys to remember the
splendor of the scenery where we first spotted them. I've seen
loons three times in Iceland: first in Steingrímsfjörður in the
west fjords, a craggy and almost uninhabited stretch of country; again at the north shore of Mývatn, where one can almost
expect to find them; and last at almost midnight from the deck
of a small fishing boat in the middle of Skagafjörður, ignoring the noisy fulmars while it floated along in solitary majesty, its melancholy hoot sounding like a ground bass under
the squawking fulmars waiting for a snack of fish guts. Since
it's the state bird of Minnesota, its voice almost—though not
quite—made me homesick.

Holtavörðuheiði is the high moor on the west coast that
separates Icelandic weather systems. It is often foggy in summer and ice- and snowbound in winter. I've come to feel almost proprietary about the family of swans who seem to
permanently inhabit a boggy pool along the high road. How
elegant those huge white swans look, shrouded in dank sea
mist on the bleak moor. Another pair of them live in what is

certainly one of the only wet and vegetated oases in the vast black desert on the eastern moors. They look even whiter, more alive, surrounded by all that dead black sand. I saw them once on a clear day. Their small bog faced Iceland's grandest and seldom-visible mountain Herðubreið (Broad Shoulders), standing alone fifty miles inland. In my occasional mystical moments, I imagine those swans as guardians of the mountain, but they very likely pay more attention to the edible creatures in the bog slime beneath them than to a big, square rock so far away.

The birder's ultimate El Dorado is the bird cliff. Iceland is rich with them: Reykjanesviti, only a few miles from the airport; Arnarstapi on Snæfellsnes; Drangey, the sheer-cliffed island six miles out the window of my house in Skagafjörður; Rauðanúpur at the northeast tip of the country; and the islands Grímsey, Skrúður, and Papey. But the two largest and most famous, Skoruvíkurbjarg and Látrabjarg, occupy the ends of long peninsulas, respectively the northeasternmost and westernmost points of Iceland. Látrabjarg is Iceland's nearest geographical approach to east Greenland—only one hundred and eighty miles away—and then North America.

In the summer of 2004, I was determined to see both Látrabjarg and Skoruvíkurbjarg. I had by then had quite enough of the United States and its idiotic war. I was tired of apologizing for being an American, and my Icelandic wasn't sufficient to convince anyone that I wasn't one. I was tired, I think, of everything but nature, literature, and Franz Joseph Haydn. I wanted to lay atop a high cliff at the very edge of the world, listening to squawking and the flapping of wings, multiplied a million times to drown out the noise on the rest of the planet. I wanted the sanity of birds, whose job is to eat, survive, and behave like themselves, who are not demented with the mania of owning things, and who do not moralize and prattle about their piddly gods.

One of my cousins, Wally Benson, nearing eighty, arrived from South Dakota with his family to see the home of the ancestors. Like so many of us westerners of Icelandic descent, Wally grew up listening to the Icelandic spoken by parents, grandparents, and neighbors, and eating midwestern versions of Icelandic food prepared mostly by women who had never set foot in Iceland: *Vinarterta*—a layered prune cake, *lifrarpylsa*—a sausage of liver, suet, and onions sewn into a cloth sack, *kleinur*—crooked doughnuts flavored with cardamom and fried crisp in hot fat, and brown bread rich with molasses and lard. All these things still existed, but in forms neither Wally nor I recognized. The vinarterta was now a dry cake with rhubarb jam, the *lifrarpylsa* lighter on suet and sewn in the sheep's intestine, and the brown bread sans lard and steamed in hot springs rather than baked. Wally arrived in Hofsós amazed to find it so green and fertile and spacious. "Pretty good farms here. . . . Why'd they leave?" he said while we were frying slices of *lifrarpylsa* in butter with a spoonful of sugar—a recipe used only by old Icelanders now. "Not enough suet. I like Ma's recipe better," commented Wally.

"Wait till we go east," I told him. "You'll see why they left." Hardly a blade of grass for fifty miles, and what there was covered by ash from a volcano. They had good reason to leave: they needed more suet, more live sheep to provide their livers, and more hay for everything alive.

I took Wally for a little birding drive on the gravel road to Bær. Godwits and redshanks lined the fence posts, the whimbrels trilled satisfactorily and pointed their beaks to scold us as they flew by, and a few ptarmigan burped out of the ditches, activating Wally's hunter's eye. The terns were, as usual, berserk, dive-bombing any intruder in sight. "I didn't think you paid any attention to this stuff, Billy," said Wally.

"I didn't, but turning sixty has made me a little smarter in that regard."

"Remember your ma's recipe for pheasant in cream?"

"I do, and *your* ma's chicken *kæfa*. I haven't eaten anything so good since she died." So meditated two old sons of Icelanders on the passage of time and the mysteries of birds, dead or alive.

The next day we set out for Vopnafjörður, the fjord that was the ancestral home for most of Minneota, Minnesota, Wally's and my hometown. It is about two hundred and fifty miles east of Hofsós. The route passes through an astonishing variety of landscape, first over a craggy mountain pass to Akureyri, the "big" town of north Iceland, and surely its most vegetated— full of trees, gardens, old wooden houses, and a properly narrow and steep fjord. It looks more like a provincial Norwegian town than Iceland. The land around it is also fertile and green, as are the rolling hills and farms extending fifty miles to the east. Then you arrive at Mývatn, a magical lake surrounded by new lava, the site of the most intense volcanic activity on the ridge that divides Iceland. The lake is calm, shallow, fed by hot springs, full of nutrients for bird and fish, the breeding ground and winter home of an astonishing variety. The air has a tang of sulphur in it, as if this lovely, pastoral place were about to explode, showering hot lava and ash. And I suppose it might.

Then the black desert, vegetation thinned to lichens and a little moss, then nothing, save conical mounds of gravel punctuated by boulders, traversed by a road lined with yellow posts for snowplow drivers and to guide cars caught in the frequent dank fogs and sandstorms. An Englishman driving this road with me once made the best laconic description of it: "Rather bleak. I wouldn't be keen to drive it again. . . ." Nor would I, but drive it I do, escorting descendants and visiting my cousin, who lives at the end of the road. I introduced Wally to what I now think of as my pet pair of swans. "What the hell do they eat here?" asked Wally sensibly. He was even more puzzled to find the occasional sheep munching on something hidden under the black gravel or licking salt from the stones.

We arrived at the sea again and found cousin Cathy and her husband Sverrir's new guest house on the farm Refsstaður II. It's a pleasant, modern house, with just a peek at the sea a scant mile away and a rich, wet meadow full of phlegmatic Icelandic dairy cows with huge, swinging milk bags. This large, green fjord of three fertile valleys is the reward for having survived the black desert. The song to accompany our joy came from a dozen whimbrels trilling—not quite in unison.

We found farms where our ancestors once lived, but few remnants of their residence. Mud and driftwood and piled stones don't last a century. Aside from cutting down the native birch woods and introducing the sheep to ungrazed landscape, the old Icelanders left little to mark their presence on this rough island. The signs of sheep, on the other hand, are always clearly visible.

Wally and his family went south over Hellisheiði (Iceland's highest mountain pass) the next day to find the Benson farms (Björnsson in its original incarnation) in Jökuldalur, a high valley buried in ash in 1875 and almost entirely vacated. I stayed on at Refsstaður with Cathy and Sverrir, my sights set on Langanes—only an hour to the north.

I first met Sverrir Ásgrímsson three years ago, after he and Cathy decided to throw in their lots together. Sverrir is a gentle, silent man, physically very strong—he spent his life working in the fish business—but not fond of large groups of chattering people. Since I am largely (though not entirely) a chatterer by nature, I tend to trust only those introverts whose mistrust of easy, sociable language means that what they do say has a real bottom to it. Fortunately, this is true of Sverrir. I asked him if he came from Vopnafjörður ætt. No, he said, from Langanes, the farm Skoruvík. He then told me about his childhood in this wild, bleak, now-uninhabited place. I wrote immediately afterward a digest of what he told me, mostly in his own words.

Sverrir at Skoruvík

Skoruvík was the last farm on the last road before the end of Langanes, the long peninsula shaped like a duck's head pointing northward. It was farther from anywhere not itself than anywhere else on this whole island, which is itself the farthest anywhere from somewhere, the apotheosis of *langt í burtu*—"far away." It was farthest from the warm Gulf Stream, closest to the icy east-Greenland current. Sea birds loved its cold cliffs and many made their home there. Gray basking sharks with sieves instead of teeth lived in this ice water, slurping tiny shrimps. The weather was always bad there, weeks of heavy clouds and sea fog, a few hours of weak sun, then again the shroud. Skoruvík was so much in the sea that wind blew from all directions at once there. We lit oil lamps, shat in an outhouse, the phone a wood box with bell and a winder and sometimes a voice at the other end. We were nine children in the little house. I loved it there and dream of it still, always close to nature. I went to school at Þórshöfn, on the duck's back.

Once, I was so lonesome at Christmas for Skoruvík that I walked seven hours north in the dark. Nothing left now: no farms, no children, no road, an empty lighthouse, and only a broken track that would break a jeep.

And the great silence and the heavy fog, and the wind blowing from all directions at once, and the crying of the gulls and gannets, and the sloshing of the cold, shark-rich sea in its last few miles before the ice takes over once and for all.

How I love that line of pure poetry: "The wind blowing from all directions at once." If that doesn't send a bleak chill down your spine, you haven't formed a mental picture yet. But the day I was there was not bleak at all. Hardly a breeze from any direction, a blue, sunlit sky, sixty-five degrees, Gunnar's cows mooing and groaning in the buttercup-strewn meadow below the deck at Refsstaður, the family of whimbrels still warbling their trills, a few sleepily buzzing flies, the sea glistening with light. "You could not possibly have better weather to see Skoruvík," said Sverrir.

"But we don't have a big jeep."

"They have fixed the road this year. We can take your car. It will be all right." Off we went, Cathy, Sverrir, and I, driving an hour north to Þórshöfn, a sleepy little fishing village on the duck's back. First we passed Gunnólfsvíkurfjall, an elegantly shaped mountain rising over two thousand feet sheer out of the sea at the bottom of Langanes. Until recently, the Americans maintained a radar station on top to monitor the Russians—now maybe al-Qaeda or the Iraqi navy—in this almost-Arctic Ocean. How silly the Cold War—or the War on Terror, or any other for that matter—seen on this day from this place. What gullible fools we humans can be.

The road continued paved out of Þórshöfn a few miles to Sauðanes (the Sheep Peninsula), with an old wood church and a nineteenth-century stone parsonage, now restored. Below the small hill down to the sea sat thousands of eider ducks waiting peacefully to have their down plucked. The funeral for Sverrir's father was held in this, his ancestral church. The paved road stopped. While it was, as Sverrir had promised, passable, it was not good. Enough stones and ruts and washouts remained to remove an oil pan should you speed. But why speed? Why rush to finish such a magical afternoon? The road wound between a boggy lagoon and the sea. The loud sky suddenly turned cloudy with kría wings—thousands of them. The sea disappeared behind ten-foot-high piles of drift logs, enough to build several of Þórshöfn. Good fishing for oyster-catchers, who lined the road in great numbers, thweeping at us with their lurid orange-pink beaks. The road rose, winding through fields of bare black stones. The land behind us disappeared, nothing but endless sea to the north.

"Are we there yet?"

"Oh, no, it is a long way still." Introverts never deceive you just to cheer you up. After the better part of an hour snaking up and down hills of boulders and through sea bogs lined with a forest of driftwood, we came to an oasis of rich, mattress-soft grass full of wildflowers atop a cliff.

"What's the shack?" I asked.

"For the egg gatherers," said Sverrir. "Stop the car here. You will smell it soon. They have fertilized the grass well."

We walked toward the lip of the cliff. I did smell it before I heard them: the rich stink of bird shit, then the loud orchestra of honks, squeals, shrieks, and snorts. Below us, maybe thousands of birds arranged in high-rise apartments on every ledge and crevasse in the cliff, wheeling and diving in a chaos of wings: guillemots, fulmars, kittiwakes, gulls, razorbills. But a hundred feet below on their own private rock—Stóri karl, the Big Fellow, a round, flat-topped column rising three hundred feet out of the sea—lived the aristocrat gannets, their round, black house now half-white with centuries of shit. They were squeezed together, those huge and powerful birds. There seemed hardly room to unfold their enormous, black-tipped wings when they raised their pale yellow heads to take off and then circle over the sea, surveying the water with their deep-set yellow eyes till they spotted a fish, maybe a hundred and fifty feet below, and plunged down like a shot arrow, rising with the hapless fish clamped in their long, gray scissor beak. What airplane could compete with these birds for splendor, ingenuity, design, or grace? How silly and pretentious they make us humans look, with our schemes and inventions! I lay in the soft grass on the cliff a long time looking at them—only a little tempted to step off the edge and try my wings.

After a while I became aware of a ledge just under the lip of the cliff where a line of guillemots had gathered. What comical-looking birds they are, with their fat white breasts and night-black tailcoats. They seemed entirely unafraid of me. I considered reaching over the cliff to pat a smooth, black head. Again, I resisted. The noise and the smell and the power of the gannets had almost drained the opinions out of me. Maybe that's the function of a proper bird cliff.

"But where is the farm Skoruvík?"

"It is still farther from here. The cliffs go on for miles. I came here often as a boy and hung from a rope to gather eggs." Sverrir chuckled with pleasure at the memory. I looked back over the cliff and shuddered at the thought of dropping at rope's end, an egg bag over my shoulder. The fat flatlander flies only in his imagination.

We bumped onward for another twenty minutes over a road now of pure stones. We rounded a bend to another oasis of grass. "This is Skoruvík," said Sverrir, "but there is nothing left. They burned the house early this summer. My bed was still there. The house was all right." Melancholy overtook him as he surveyed the bulldozed heap of burned rubble, all that re-mained of a childhood that, despite its poverty and isolation, gave him his joy in nature. "And here was the old storage shed where we kept potatoes." We stepped over a half-dozen kinds of wildflowers blooming in the sun-warmed grass. All three of us stared out straight north at the sea—the vast infinity of water that from here ended only at the polar ice, the next true landfall probably the north coast of Alaska. I tried to imagine the three hundred and fifty days a year of fog, blustering wind, and blizzards, but on a day like that you would forgive the gods everything. I walked over to the rubble heap to begin gathering detritus: a rusty square nail, a dried sheep bone, a charred piece of wood, a shard of patterned white stucco siding. "And here is a splinter from Sverrir's bed, and a sheep bone he gnawed as a child, and a nail from the door to his room." My cousin Cathy, who has known me for fifty years, is never surprised by my eccentricities. Sverrir just harrumphed. But though he would deny it, I contend that an introvert's true feeling is visible always in his body, in his face, and for those few moments in the sun at his old farm, Sverrir was cast down like D. H. Lawrence under his mother's piano "in the flood of remembrance," with "the glamour of childish days" upon him. What is the shame for human beings to weep at the passage of time and to feel it in the disappearance of the objects of our past? These emotions give us all literature and music and art. They give us our humanity.

We turned to return back down the duck's head to Þórshöfn—forty kilometers, twenty-five miles. Just past the bird cliff on a high knob, I spotted an unusual rock near the road. It looked as if someone had piled yet another rock atop the boulder, but no—the three of us said in unison, in whatever language—*falcon*. There sat a handsome one not fifty feet from the windshield, posing still as a statue. My first falcon. I felt something akin to what the birders in Skagafjörður felt: awe, wonder, humility, even, in the presence of this fierce beauty.

He sat there for a minute or two, letting us watch him until he spotted something more clearly killable and edible than the three stunned humans in the car. When he rose into the air on his swift wings, I thought of Hopkins watching the windhover, the English name for the falcon:

> I caught this morning morning's minion,
>   Kingdom of daylight's dauphin, dapple-dawn-drawn
>   Falcon, in his riding
>   Of the rolling level underneath him steady air, and
>   striding
>   High there, how he rung upon the rein of a
>   wimpling wing
>   In his ecstasy! then off, off forth on swing,
>   As a skate's heel sweeps smooth on a bow-bend: the
>   hurl and gliding
>   Rebuffed the big wind. My heart in hiding
>   Stirred for a bird,—the achieve of, the mastery of
>   the thing!

When he was gone, we exhaled and said to each other in our own way—what a gift we have received. What a grand finish to a fine day. But in fact the day was not over yet.

We drove on over the crest of the hill, maybe a hundred yards, very slowly. "My god!" we said again in unison, not even needing to identify what stood before us in the middle of the road, as if he were carved from solid granite, not twenty feet away. It was a white-tailed eagle, largest and perhaps rarest of all Icelandic birds. There was no mistaking it—he was too mammoth to be anything else, with a white tail, the hooked beak, and—how else to say it?—the eagle eye. Like the falcon, he sat stock-still for several minutes, eyeing us. Cathy leaned out the front window to take his picture. "Is he hurt?" she asked.

Finally he moved, awkwardly waddling as if his body were too heavy to become airborne, like an overloaded cargo plane that couldn't quite summon the power to rise on takeoff. Then he began to unfurl those eight- or nine-foot-wide wings to catch an updraft. When the wind caught him, truly, he soared. Again we looked at each other, dumbfounded. What next? Christ come again in glory to judge the quick and the dead? The ghost of the last great auk? A condor far from home? We drove on, now back through the familiar kría swarm, to Þórshöfn, where we stopped to have an ice cream and a hot dog at the Esso station and to rinse a little Langanes dust off the windows for the ride home—to reenter the ordinary world which, after that afternoon, no longer seemed so ordinary.

ELVES OUT THE WINDOWS

The world out the windows of Brimnes looks like a construction project that has run out of funds. The mountains are giant mud-and-scree heaps that have slid down toward the sea but not quite arrived. On the mud shelves at the mountain's foot are a few houses and barns that seem to be only temporary, until the next slide. The islands and headlands rearing up from the water look in need of five hundred or a thousand years of vigorous erosion and polishing to smooth their rough surfaces. The cliffs, stark black but for great, uneven streaks of seabird shit, could use some cosmic hose to clean and shine them. From my window, the sea-facing cliff on the headland Þórðarhöfði appears to be sheer and symmetrical, a stern right angle. It is about four miles to the north. I sailed past it once and found it gnarled, tortured, twisted, and fractured, like Edvard Munch's *The Scream* hammered out by a blind, bad-tempered monster. At the cliff top (202 meters, 650 feet up) is a volcanic crater. Þórðarhöfði is an unfinished lava sculpture, the ghost, if you like, of the relatively recent eruption that made it. The peak of the cliff is called Herkonuklettur (Warriorwoman Cliff). Two hollows below it are called Skessuspor—the Trollwoman's Footprints. A trollwoman left them while taking a shortcut through Skagafjörður. On the south face of the headland stand several basalt columns called Búðarbrekkur (the Shop Slope). Local lore has it that this is the church, shop, and dwelling of the elves. Somewhat over three sections (square miles) of grass, lichen, bare rock, in the past grazed by sheep and horses—and, of course, by elves—the headland is connected to mainland Skagafjörður by two narrow gravel isthmuses, just wide enough for a horse track or a walking path. Behind it lies Höfðavatn, a six-and-a-half square mile freshwater lake teeming with sweet trout. Maybe the elves prefer freshwater fish.

Across the highway from Þórðarhöfði and a mile to the south is the ancient farmstead Þrastastaðir. I know it well because my friend Valgeir was raised there, and his parents, now nearly eighty, Valdi and Didda (Þórvaldur and Valgerður, to be precisely formal) still live and farm there. The farm has a fine view of the whole fjord, including the blazing, surreal sunsets, from its slightly elevated perch on the mud slope below a big mountain. Imagine my surprise at finding that the following adventure happened to their medieval predecessor on the same farm:

Thórdur of Thrastastadir

A certain man named Thórdur lived at Thrastastadir, in Skagafjörður.

One day, in the winter, he started from home, intending to go to the trading town of Hofsós, but the snow had drifted so deeply that the way was thought unsafe. Not caring for this, he carried his merchandise in a bag and walked off across a bog, which he knew to be his shortest path to Hofsós. When he had gone a little way, he quite lost the track, but still walked straight on till nightfall, when he saw before him some warehouses, so lofty and so beautiful that they filled him with surprise. Going up to them he discovered a light in one of the windows, and at the same time heard some delightful music. So he looked in at the window and saw a number of people dancing. He then went to the door and knocked, and immediately it was opened by a well-dressed man, who asked him what he would? Thórdur told him how he had lost his way, and begged, if it were possible, for a night's shelter.

"Come in and be welcome," said the man, "you shall have shelter here. Bring in your bag too, and tomorrow I will trade with you, and I promise you that you shall not find the bargains of Hofsós better than mine."

Thórdur could scarcely believe his ears, but thought he must be dreaming. So the man let him into the chief room, in spite of Thórdur's plain and muddy dress. There were many assembled there: the lady of the house, her children, and her servants, all gaily and brightly drest, making merry.

The man who had opened the door to Thórdur, and who was no other than the master of the house, said to the lady, "Wife, here is a man who has lost his way and who needs both rest and food: treat him well."

"I grieve to hear of his distress," replied she, and rising, brought in a good and plentiful supper, which she set before Thórdur, while the master of the house fetched wine and glasses, and begged Thórdur to drink with him. Thórdur did so, and thought he had never tasted such wine in all his life, nor ever met such goodly company, though he could not, for all that, help wondering at the strangeness of the adventure. Glass after glass of wine he drank, and by-and-by, becoming tipsy, went to bed and fell into a deep sleep.

Next morning, at breakfast, he was offered wine even better than that of the night before, and having drunk it, was conducted by the master to the trading room, which was well filled with every kind of merchandise. Then and there Thórdur showed the man his wares, and received from him in exchange more than half again what he would have got for them at Hofsós. With the money he bought corn and linen, and many other small things, at a much lower price than he was wont to pay elsewhere for the like, and filled with them his sack.

When the trading was finished the master offered him as a gift, a cloak for his wife and cakes for his children, saying to him, "These and many other good turns shall you have at my hands, as tokens of my gratitude to you for having saved my son from death." Thórdur wondered what the man could mean, but the other said, "Once, you were standing under the rock called Thórdarhöfdi, in company with other young men, waiting for a good wind to take your boat to Drangey. Your companions amused themselves by throwing stones against the rock, under which, as the sun was very hot, my son had laid himself down to sleep; for he was tired, having been up all the night. You bade them cease their sport, for it was a foolish one, you said, and useless. They laughed at you for this notion of yours, and called you strange and fanciful for your pains. But had you not prevented them from throwing stones, they would have killed my son."

After this Thórdur took leave of all in the house, for the sky was now clear and the path good, and started on his homeward way, the master walking some steps with him, to wish him "Godspeed." Thórdur marched on steadily for a while; but chancing to look back for the house wherein he had passed the night, he saw nothing of it, but, in its place, the rocks of the Thórdarhöfdi. Then he understood that the kind merchant was an elf, and hastening home, told his wife all that had befallen him, and gave her the cloak. As for the wares he had got instead of his own, he showed them to all his neighbors, and never were the like of them, for goodness, seen in all that country, nor in any other country under the sun.

It is peculiar for a Minnesotan to live in a place where the geographical steps of such stories can be easily traced. I know those marshes. I know how possible it is to be lost in a blizzard there. I look at the elves' black mansion every day. They have never offered me fine wine or a good dinner—or, for that matter, a good price for my poems—but then on the other hand, I didn't unknowingly save an elf boy from death. I suppose the moral of the story is that we ought to be more careful when we see our fellows behaving brutally or stupidly. Stop that! Don't you dare! After all, an old elf may be watching.

The book from which this legend is drawn is a real treasure. It should be reprinted in facsimile, along with its twenty-eight magnificent etchings—a giant's fist coming down a chimney, an uneasy skeleton in an old church (Hólar, also nearby), an elf army on their miniature horses, two monster horses joined at the rump, a woman galloping on horseback to church on Christmas Eve, behind her dead lover's bare skull. What a rich breeding ground this spare landscape is for the imagination. No trees, no crops, and few wild animals; a long, black winter followed by cold, foggy, blustery summers; a few scattered people and a few old farms now half-wrecked and deserted. But this relatively barren setting provides nicely for an enormous population of elves, ghosts, monsters, and sorcerers—nature itself is haunted everywhere.

The big mountain out the front window, Tindastóll, is particularly rich in weird lore. At Glerhallavík, on the north end of the mountain, a magic wishing stone from a well floats to the surface every midsummer night (June twenty-first). In the cove Baulubás is Bauluhellir—Cow Cave, so named because cows walked through it from a valley in the next fjord to the east. It is the home of sea monsters. Tindastóll is, of course, home to giants and trolls (not kindly elves). In the Middle Ages, a giant kidnapped the bishop's daughter from Hólar, just across the fjord, and kept her in his cave for a long time. She was never quite the same after that. Drangey, the cliff island a mile or two in front of Tindastóll, houses an evil spirit who will shred the ropes you dangle from over the sea. The evil one speaks in a low, gravelly voice.

Just north of Þórðarhöfði, the rocky peninsula Sléttuhlíð juts out into the fjord. There's an old church on the farm Fell, served in the sixteenth century by Rev. Hálfdán Narfason, a famous sorcerer. His sister Hildigunn lived at Lónkot, a coastal farm that is now a resort just south of Fell. Her son Björn was Hálfdán's servant in sorcery. To break a spell cast by a powerful troll on a local girl, Hálfdán sent Björn thirty miles north across the sea to the island Grímsey, the whole way riding a peculiar horse: an enchanted human thighbone. Björn's only comment when he saw what he'd been riding across the water was that he had little to say in its favor, but clearly, it had not been corn-fed. They summoned the troll (named Bergfinn), who reluctantly released Valdís, the girl, from the spell, after which nephew Björn, the bone rider, married her.

The island Málmey, about two and a half miles long and surrounded by rugged cliffs, but a good farm because topped with rich grass, lies a few miles out in the fjord west of Sléttuhlíð. The island's curse was that any farmwife who stayed there over twenty years disappeared. The island was farmed until 1950, though never with long-dwelling wives. During Hálfdán's curacy, farmer Jón defied the spell, and, predictably, his wife disappeared—as if into thin air. Jón went to Hálfdán for help. The pastor was not anxious to assist, but he finally agreed. He saddled his gray horse in the churchyard, inviting Jón to sit behind him but cautioning him, in peril of his life, not to speak a word. Off they rode east, almost with flying hooves, to the mountain in the next fjord, Ólafsfjarðarmúli, a two-thousand-foot cliff falling straight to the sea. Hálfdán knocked at a rock on the cliff face with his rod. Two women in blue came out, leading a third—Jón's wife, now swollen and bluish, with the mark of the baptismal cross on her forehead to identify her. She asked Jón what he wanted. Hálfdán asked Jón if he wanted her back. He shook his head, and they returned on horseback to Sléttuhlíð. For the next five hundred years, no one dared keep a wife on Málmey. Now it is empty, except when my neighbors go there in spring to harvest the delicious seabird eggs. Rev. Hálfdán closed the rock behind him with his rod so it can never again be opened. That rock in the cliff is red, unlike all the surrounding black. It has since been known as Hálfdánarhurð—Hálfdán's Door.

On the west side of the fjord, after Tindastóll ends, is the marshy lowland at the end of the Skagi Peninsula. On the farm Keta—almost visible out my window on a clear day—is the rock Grímsborg, famous as the home of numerous "hidden people," or elves, who have often come to the aid of those in distress.

Who are the elves? One day God came to visit Adam and Eve. They greeted him, probably offered him coffee, and showed off their house. God wanted to see the children, so they showed them off too. God thought they looked promising, and asked Eve if she had any more. No, she lied. As a good Icelandic housewife, she was ashamed that she hadn't finished washing some of the children, so she hid them. God (who, like Odin, knows things—maybe he has his ravens, too?) was not pleased. He said that whatever Adam and Eve hid from him would be forever hidden from men. Those children's descendants, now invisible to mankind, became the elves, who live in rocks, cliffs, and hummocks scattered across Iceland. We, on the other hand, are the descendants of clean children—our ætt. The elves can always see us, but we can see them only rarely, if they allow it.

These elves are not the "little people," the cute felt and pottery *huldufólk* in gift shops, nor grotesque dwarves with buckteeth, big noses, silly grins, and pointy shoes. They are the mirror of us, what a Jungian might call the shadow self, or the interior life. The stories about them are not whimsy or fantasy, but rather coded messages—hidden wisdom—to be revealed to us when we exercise our "second sight." Indeed, some seem more gifted with this second sight than others. A piano teacher in Hafnarfjörður sees hidden people continuously, has even published a map showing the locations of the stones and gullies that house them. Road construction crews are careful to avoid laying roadbeds through elf dwellings. Many stories circulate of road accidents caused by ignoring elves. Icelanders surveyed by pollsters prove themselves overwhelmingly rational and skeptical—but then on the other hand, of course, there are stories, and many believe in them. . . . I don't myself, but when I was gardening in my new place, this particular stone was cracked oddly. . . . Icelanders seem by instinct to subscribe to W. B. Yeats's famous old line about the fairies: "Everything is true, and the earth is only a little dust under our feet." The same Icelander, even an occasional churchgoer and no declared atheist, who would tell you that the virgin birth, the loaves and fishes, and the resurrection are only stories for children, believes wholeheartedly in the literal truth of the sagas—"Of course, Grettir's head lies under that boulder"—and is quite open to the presence of elves, hauntings, mischievous *mori* (family ghosts who haunt a whole ætt), and places in nature mysteriously blessed or cursed.

The half-finished landscape, the bareness, the volcanic and smoking earth, the loneliness of such vast stretches, the extended darkness in winter and the long, strange light of summer: all contribute to a rich terrain for the supernatural. It is perhaps notable that the number of stories declined with the advent of electricity in Reykjavík, and then across the country. The haunted spots in nature seemed to bury their ghosts when paved, high-speed roads were built in the last twenty-five years. I remember marvelous stories of a ghostly hitchhiker on Holtavörðuheiði, the much-traveled high moor that separates north from south Iceland. He would sit in the backseat, talking brilliantly, but when you let him out (always on the moor) he appeared in the rearview mirror holding his head under his arm. Now, of course, you can drive over the moor at seventy miles an hour on a fine, safe road, with a digital monitor at both ends telling you the wind speed, temperature, and road condition ahead. But years ago, one seldom drove the rough gravel track without getting stuck, breaking an axle, or losing an oil pan. The hidden people must not be friends of modern technology and progress.

Why did the emigrants not bring these stories with them? In either their immigrant chests or in their heads? The stories connect directly to the peculiarity of nature and landscape in Iceland, an empty place when they began settling it in 874. These tales arise from the ancient tales of Norse mythology seen in a new place, and then developed further with the graft of Christianity onto the old myths. The fit is often uncomfortable—for example, Hálfdán the Sorcerer-Priest—but the peculiar energy in the stories comes from the inescapable friction between these two sources. Notice that God visiting Eve behaves like a district chieftain visiting one of his vassal farms. In North America the Icelanders arrived in a place already settled—and vastly more modern than the farms they had left. The railroad, the tall buildings, the wild animals, the teeming cities—even the vast fields of wheat and corn (called maize by the Icelanders)—probably seemed almost supernatural as well. The Icelandic emigrants to both Canada and the United States seem to have been more interested in and gotten along better with their Native neighbors than with other groups. And not surprisingly: after all, the Indians are the Icelanders of North America. They alone possess the ancient folklore, nature, religion, and intimate connection of landscape, culture, and daily life. The rest of us—Icelandic emigrants included, of course—are only Johnny-come-latelies to the North American continent. If the local hidden people make themselves known, it will more likely be to a wandering Cree or Ojibwa, not to an upstart Scandinavian. The first Icelanders on Lake Winnipeg were starving after the lake froze solid. They'd never fished under ice till the Cree, in a neighborly gesture, taught them how to do it. A famous, much-repeated story tells of an Icelander from the old country meeting an Indian north of Winnipeg who addressed him in perfectly good Icelandic. Where in god's name did he learn Icelandic? I don't speak Icelandic, said the man, only Húnavatnsslumál— the home county in Iceland of great numbers of emigrants. All history is local, I suppose, including ghosts and elves.

Today I sit staring out the windows of Brimnes at a white snake of fog half-covering Tindastóll's giant caves and magic springs. Still more gray mist and drizzle fill the air. My head is filled with supernatural neighbors. Countless elf and ghost sites are either visible out this window or only a mile or two away by car or foot. This is my haunted, temporary turf, and I like it that way: every rock and bog with its story.

THE MELANCHOLY QUOTIENT

I begin my sixties with the melancholy understanding that I am, finally, without any aunts or uncles. My last aunt—my mother's youngest sister, Kristín Júlíana Hermansdóttir Josephson Waters, called Stína—died in Braintree, Massachusetts at a few months past ninety-one. Stína was born in the back room of a farmhouse in Westerheim Township, Minnesota, in February 1912 to her mother, my grandmother Kristín Júlíana Þórðardóttir (after whom she was named), and to Herman Vigfússon Josephson. My grandmother was forty-three years old at the time, only ten years in the New World. She emigrated from Þingeyjarsýsla in north Iceland in 1902, arriving first in Winnipeg. My grandfather Herman's first wife (and first cousin), Aðalbjörg, died bearing my uncle Aðalbjorn in 1904—the seventh pregnancy of her marriage. Herman spoke a little rough English (though he had been in Minnesota since 1879) but was ill-equipped to care for what were then five living children aged from eleven to newborn. Herman, born in 1859 on a farm next to the Sel River in the far east of Iceland, emigrated at the age of twenty with his parents, brothers, cousins, uncles, aunts, and well over half the population of his district, Vopnafjörður. In 1904, he was forty-five years old, already bowlegged, bent, one-eyed, and (rare among Icelandic emigrants) close to illiterate. No dreamboat. Though he died a month and a year before my birth in August 1943, his reputation for quick temper, quarrelsomeness, and a taste for strong drink survived him. But he was also remembered as a good (though never rich) farmer, an honest dealer, and a ruthless worker who flew into rages at the mere thought of idleness. His farm was probably not a good residence for dreamers, poets, or mystics. Herman was not a church member and disliked religion. His children were married in the backyard, though the Icelandic preacher got paid his pittance. He disliked foreigners more than he disliked Christianity, and the *prestur* at least spoke Icelandic.

My grandmother Kristín arrived in Winnipeg at the age of thirty-two, unmarried but guardian and surrogate mother for her ten-year-old cousin, Árni. Árni's parents were either early dead, lepers (common in that district in the nineteenth century), or so sunk in poverty that they couldn't feed their boy. Kristín was herself only a single rung up that ladder of poverty. She worked as a "hired girl" on a farm south of Húsavík, the lowest social and legal status possible in Iceland. She owned nothing except a few books, one of which, Séra Hallgrímur Pétursson's *Passion Psalms*, she knew by heart and recited to herself one a day for the forty days of Lent. They are not small poems. Knowing them is like having the equivalent of two or three plays by Shakespeare rolling around in your head. Unlike Herman, she was neither illiterate nor did she dislike Christianity (though like most Icelanders she was no churchgoer—real religion was a private matter, with church providing only the marking of passages: baptism, confirmation, funeral, and sometimes Christmas).

She was certainly not a trophy wife. Aside from owning nothing, having care of a small boy, and being (in nineteenth-century terms) already old, she was no great beauty. Like Herman, she had a glass eye, a squat body, heavy features, and a tight bun stuffed with already-graying hair.

Herman traveled in 1905 to Winnipeg—about four hundred and fifty miles north of his farm—to meet her, on the advice of one of his cousins who farmed not far from the city. He probably told Herman something like this: "She just got off the boat, no money, no prospects, looks in need of work and a place to live." Herman intended to hire her as housekeeper, cook, and tender of children. He had quite enough mouths to feed already. But Kristín, though no prize catch, was possessed of a true Icelandic ego. She told Herman that she had no intention of raising his children on some godforsaken farm miles from town for a mere pittance and room and board. She would come to Minneota with him only as his wife. She was much younger and intended to outlive him, inherit part of the farm, and enjoy a serene old age, knitting, humming, and reciting Séra Hallgrímur's poems to herself whenever she pleased. Left little choice, Herman married her and she came south with him, undoubtedly an illegal immigrant, to become my grandmother.

I never met her. She died in 1933 of peritonitis from an impacted bowel. She was sixty-three, and failed in her hope to outlive the already seventy-four-year-old Herman. He lasted another decade, tough as old saddle leather and quarrelsome to the end. My aunt Stína, the youngest of the children, told me that her mother, on her deathbed, was full of bitterness—not only at her too early and painful death but also at not achieving her dream of spending Herman's inheritance in her own little house in Minneota, surrounded by other old Icelandic ladies who, like her, failed ever to learn or speak a word of English.

I doubt whether Herman or Kristín ever used the word or even entertained the notion of "love" in our modern romantic sense. If ever there were a marriage of pure practicality, it was theirs. However, the absence of romance didn't inhibit them from having four further children in quick succession: Aunt Sigthora in 1906, Uncle Herman in 1908, my mother Jonina Sigurborg in 1910, and the last, little Stína, in 1912. Then

Herman at fifty-three and Kristín at forty-two retired from child rearing for good, aside from bringing up their daughter Sigthora's child, Clifford, conceived out of wedlock and fatherless, from 1924 until 1933. Adding Kristín's young cousin Árni into the mix (he was reared up as one of the children) brought the number of children in her care to ten.

I knew most of them. In the first batch were August (1893), Josef (1895), Rose (1898), Lilja (1900), and Aðalbjorn—Abo—(1904), with a couple of infant deaths spaced between. Rose died of Spanish flu just after World War I, and I only vaguely remember meeting Lilja, who escaped from Minneota to Minneapolis. She worked for the railroad as a secretary and died unmarried of a combination of tuberculosis and cancer in 1948. Uncle Joe, a silent man, disappeared to Nebraska and seldom appeared in Minneota. August, Abo, and Herman farmed, all in the near vicinity of Minneota. Jona married my father, Bill Holm, who farmed nearby, but Sigthora and Stína both married Irishmen, moved to Boston, and—horrors!—turned Catholic.

Stína's six children were born in quick succession, from 1945 to 1950. She lived in a difficult marriage with little money in a tiny cottage on the sea east of Boston, and after her pregnancies my mother traveled east to help out with the other children. Twice I came with her on the streamlined train that once connected Minneapolis and Boston. We slept in a Pullman car where, at four or five, I met my first Negro—a kind porter who would tuck in the fat little redheaded boy and pat him on the head good night. I remember his deep voice and his elegant, crisply pressed white shirt and uniform. My father, in his frayed, striped overalls decorated with various manures and grease splotches, looked nothing like this. I remember wanting to ask the porter to adopt me so I could live on this beautiful train, eating my dinner off heavy pewter dishes on a thick linen tablecloth with a cut flower in a bud vase, and not on some dismal, stinky farm buried in snowdrifts.

My two Catholic aunts made a nice contrast. Sigthora— Auntie Sig—was a powerful and aggressive woman, a great talker and teller of tales, always firmly convinced that her version of events was correct. My mother was much like that herself, and when she and Sig differed on matters of religion— who was to blame for what, and the nature of what actually happened—sparks, to put it mildly, filled the air. It ill-behooved any bystander to take sides, be they husband, son, or sister. Stína, the youngest of the three daughters of Kristín, was also the shortest by three or four inches, and the only introvert among them. She was always called "Little Stína," even when the three of them were old. She seldom got the chance to finish sentences or to interject her version of events when the three of them gathered together. Their verbal energy was simply too much for her.

Her revenge, though that is too strong a word for it, was to outlive both of them by a couple of decades. I went to visit her at intervals of a year or two toward the end of her life and found, a little to my surprise, that she was as gifted a wit and storyteller as her older sisters and had her own view of events, which was often quite different from theirs. They had simply overwhelmed her with volume, speed, and a failure to listen (a failure quite common among the Josephsons, as it is in so many families). But in her long and mostly serene old age, she prevailed. Her version became *ex cathedra*—the horse's mouth.

Looking at old pictures of Herman and Kristín next to pictures of their three daughters as young women always puzzled me. What could possibly be the genetic connection between these people? Bowlegged, mustachioed Herman with a take-no-prisoners expression and Kristín with her rumpled clothes and stoic, fishlike face, were about five feet three apiece, poor specimens at best. A pair of eyes and a pair of marbles between them. Then the daughters: my red-haired mother, blond Sig, both about five feet eight, and shorter Stína, all "lookers," as was said in those days—big, sturdy, handsome girls, all prizes for the neighborhood fellows. How did those two hatch these three? Plus my reasonably handsome uncles, Abo and Herman? Surely New World air, fresh sweet corn, and beef steaks didn't perk up the DNA stock that much that quickly. Here too then, as in so many families, a mystery.

Now Stína is gone, and I am bereft of Josephsons. Their mates are dead, and the children are beginning to die, too. Unless some damn fool writer tells the family secrets, they will soon disappear into the oblivion of history. And what confidence have you that whatever version you hear of these stories, or judgments of these characters, is accurate—much less true? Of such fine threads is all our history spun, whether human, national, civilizational, or even planetary. One sees such matters clearly out the windows of Brimnes.

My cousin Bill Cassidy sent me a note from Massachusetts a year or two ago.

> We're cleaning out Cliff's house in the process of selling it and I found some old pictures you might be interested in. I already received my melancholy quotient out of them and hope you do the same.

What an eerily curious phrase: melancholy quotient. I'm not sure how I felt about having it wished on me. But it descended nevertheless as I looked at the pictures.

Cliff Cassidy, Bill's father, who died at eighty in 2004, was, I suppose, as close to a brother as an only child will ever claim, though we never lived in the same house at the same time. Cliff was the child of my mother's older sister, Sigthora, and a traveling salesman. He was born in 1924, a great scandal then, though not much of one now. His seventeen-year-old mother had gone to a dance in Canby. There was a lawsuit, and Cliff's father was identified and made to pay up—presumably some small amount for Cliff's keeping. Sigthora left to travel and have a life away from her narrow-minded hometown, and Cliff was raised on the farm by his grandparents—in Icelandic. His grandmother died in 1933, just when my mother, Jona, married Bill Holm and settled on a nearby farm. My parents took Cliff to live with them and raised him as if he were their son.

I didn't arrive till 1943, and by that time Cliff had gone east to live in Boston with his mother and her Irish Boston husband, Bill Cassidy. Cliff was a brilliant student, both in high school and at Harvard, but his education was interrupted—like that of so many others—by World War II. Cliff was on leave and in uniform when he first saw the new baby in Bill and Jona's farm house, his half-surrogate little brother. He finished a Ph.D. in clinical psychology after the war—Dr. Cassidy, indeed!—and practiced psychology for years in various places, last in Massachusetts. My parents were inordinately proud of him—the first formally educated scion of their immigrant family. More pictures of Cliff than of me adorned our farmhouse: graduating from high school, college, graduate school, handsome in uniform, marrying. We often joked that we were an odd pair of almost brothers—me six feet five, pink and plump, Cliff five feet six, handsome and athletic, with a small circle of prematurely snow white hair on his otherwise blond head. He finished his Ph.D. I didn't, much to my mother's chagrin. She wanted another doctor, even of the phony kind. And now I've outlived him. There's a melancholy quotient for you.

The photos Cliff's son sent are the usual family snapshots—
the sort cleaned out by the shovel load from the houses of
those who have lived long. Few scribble names or occasions
or dates on the back of their snapshot collection, thus hastening the trip to the dumpster. Sometimes even names don't
help, because any people to whom those faces meant anything are themselves dead. In this case, I remember everyone.
There's a picture of the maybe ten-year-old Clifford dressed
in his Sunday best: wool knickers, long argyle socks, polished
oxfords, long-sleeved white shirt and necktie, hair carefully
combed. Next to him stands my twenty-four- or twenty-five-
year-old mother, rather elegantly dressed, white shoes, silk
stockings, a dark dress with a fancy collar, red hair tightly
curled. They stand in front of a fine-looking Model T, probably
my father's. In the background is my grandfather Herman's
barn. 1934, '35 maybe. America depressed, but Jona and Cliff
looking scrubbed, pert, cheerful.

The next picture was probably taken in 1950, a Thanksgiving
dinner in my Uncle Herman's farmhouse dining room. The
house was built by his (and Jona's) father, Herman, around
1900. My grandmother arrived in 1905. My mother was born
in the upstairs bedroom in 1910. Grandpa Herman died in the
same room in 1942—and his son Herman thirty-six years later, in
1978. In the photo, everyone has looked up from dinner to face
the camera. Nobody's dolled up. These are non-churchgoing
farmers. Herman and his wife, Blanche, and son Jim sit on the
left. Herman is in his white long johns and high boots. On the
right Little Bill, mother Jona (still the only well-dressed one),
and Gus Peterson, Blanche's father, a carpenter, maybe seventy
and often drunk—when he would stay at our farm. I thought
highly of him. He was full of tales and wisdom. My father, Big
Bill, turns around at the center to face the camera—probably
on orders from the photographer. He's wearing khaki pants,

Romeo slippers, and a plaid flannel shirt. His back and shoulders look enormous and powerful. He was a famously strong man. His hair is already gray, white at the temples; he's about forty-five. He's grinning slyly. His big head, pale to start with, is windburned dark red and brown. His neck was red from life in the fields—but not his opinions. I am the only one in this picture still alive. Cliff, not there for the family dinner, probably got a copy of the snapshot in the mail and hung on to it for the next fifty-four years. Now it's home again—though I may leave it in Iceland to show the wall what the first generation of immigrant children looked like on this American holiday. Almost certainly there was no turkey in sight; no one liked it. Both my father and Herman shot wild geese—other immigrants winging over the planet, bound for who knows where.

There are another half-dozen pictures in the melancholy packet, but you already know the drill. All dead. You have pictures of your own to match them.

In Hofsós, the main industry is genealogy—what the Icelanders call *ættfræði*. Though the locals still fish, farm, fix cars, sew flags, teach school, and count change, the larger world—mostly Canada, the United States, and Iceland itself, but also some remarkably strange and unexpected places like Brazil!—arrives here at the Vesturfarasetrið (the Icelandic Emigration Center) to put names, faces, dates, and facts on their own individual versions of the melancholy quotient. Iceland is luckier than most places because of the Icelandic mania for record keeping, a contained historical time frame from 874 until now, and a population small and homogeneous enough to make sleuthing manageable. I cannot imagine, however, any place on earth that doesn't have some version of Hofsós—a place where you can come to try to reconstruct lost history. Go back far enough and we are all emigrants. The human race has never mastered the art of staying put for long. But Hofsós is a particularly good exemplar for all such centers of genealogy, because it is small and thus can be grasped—though names disappear from faces here as rapidly as anywhere else.

Hofsós has been a marked place on maps, first an old Viking trading port, since at least the fifteenth century, probably before. It's at the mouth of one of the several rivers on the east side of Skagafjörður, with good anchorages and wind protection. Like all such places here, it fell under the control of the Danish commercial monopoly from the seventeenth until the late nineteenth century, and the rapacity of those merchants and that system exacerbated the emigration of all my relatives. The merchants bought cheap, sold dear, offered wormy flour, coffee half-chicory, moldy prunes, warped boards, and dull fishhooks. For a century or two it was a capital crime to try trading with any but your assigned factor, who charged and paid what he pleased. The old country store—the *Kaupfélag*—stood almost in ruins at the harbor's edge in Hofsós only twenty years ago.

Valgeir Þorvaldsson imagined a restored old harbor town in Hofsós (though cleaned up and sans the Danes), a museum exhibit in the old Kaupfélag (now elegantly restored), showing the causes and the results of the emigrant experience, and finally a library suited particularly for the pursuit of genealogy—books of course, but also computers full of relative-tracking software. And so he did it. It's now a lovely and useful place, joined by two fine new exhibit halls built in the old style. There's a wall of unidentified brown-tone photos of lost faces, with questions clearly implied: "Who are these people? Do you know them? Your relatives?" Now and then, one of the photos comes down; some long-dead face has gotten lucky.

Each summer brings a steady parade of visitors. The English speakers come from Canada and the United States, clutching papers covered with misspelled names, brittle yellow news clippings of obituaries, and sometimes envelopes of pictures. They are often incapable even of pronouncing their grand-parents' names or the farm name, so completely has the Icelandic language disappeared. Some know a few words. An occasional old one (usually a small-town Canadian) is still fluent, though with an archaic vocabulary. The Icelanders, of course, still have the language, but in some cases they have fewer clues as to where their century-gone relatives disap-peared to. There was little communication—and probably little love—between the old country and the new. Those who stayed often thought those who left cowards, deserters, even traitors. Those who left were often so embittered by the gross poverty, humiliation, failure, disease, and contempt that they wanted no ghosts to follow them across the Atlantic. But a century gone by is good balm for these passions, and leaves in its wake a more attractive human habit: curiosity.

Who were these people? Am I like them? What did I in-herit? Not money in the case of Iceland, but bodies, even diseases and infirmities, noses, flat feet, weak eyes, height, musical or literary talent, and, of course, habits of mind, those windows forever coloring our perceptions.

Every Icelandic story, whether the ancient sagas or the lively gossip around the coffee table, begins with the ritual chroni-cling of the *ætt*—family history. From my window at Brimnes, I look out at half the sights of *Grettir's Saga*. Our local hero was an outlaw for twenty years, a profoundly unlucky man, first lazy, then violent, finally hounded to the top of the high-cliffed island Drangey, a few miles out in the fjord. There, about a thousand years ago, Grettir was ambushed, butchered, and beheaded. Some Icelanders refer to him as if these details had just appeared in the *New York Times* or *People* magazine. The saga begins not where Grettir was born, on a farm south of Miðfjörður, two fjords west, but rather in Norway, the old country, a century before emigration here, and with the recitation of his ancestry: Onund Tree-Foot (his leg was cut off in a Viking raid), son of Ofeig Club-Foot, son of Ivar the Prick, uncle of Guðbrand Hump, father of Asta, mother of St. Olaf. The first thirteen chapters of *Grettir's Saga* are at once family gossip and history; an American might see a resemblance to adventures on the Overland Trail to California and the West. They chronicle the emigration to Iceland—who got what land where and who married into whose family. Finally little Grettir arrives in chapter 14, and the real action begins.

How can you know human character without knowing human ancestry? What good is history itself if you can't identify relatives? The closest American example I've seen of this habit of mind lives in the south. I once stopped for a day or two in Vicksburg, Mississippi and met Gordon Cotton, the museum curator, and his secretary, an elegant, blue-haired lady with, it goes without saying, a first-class genteel Mississippi accent. I remember her name as Blanche. For two days I sat listening to Gordon's and Blanche's tales of the history of the district: its plantations (some in disrepair, some not), its families, its rascals and heroes. For them, the Civil War seemed to have taken place the day before yesterday. I half-expected Jefferson Davis to appear, take his seat at the table, and raise a glass. Even a century or two ago, history was contemporary and human sized. It existed simultaneously with the present because you knew the ætt of the actors. That Mississippi history was not a dry recitation of fact, statistic, and dates. It was a tale: a narrative, story, saga. These people could have been medieval Icelanders. Maybe they were. Who knows? Later I went to Faulkner's Oxford to browse around, but that was the world of literature. Gordon Cotton's Vicksburg was living family history—as indeed history happens even now inside

Faulkner's books, because his genius (as with the author of *Grettir*) creates the illusion of life.

Lest you imagine this a white southern phenomenon, I hasten to remind you that genealogy occupies, if anything, an even larger space in black consciousness. I taught at the Hampton Institute (one of the oldest African American colleges) in the early seventies, and I recall sitting at faculty tea parties, listening with delight to family sagas—again recited mostly by elderly, elegant black ladies. These sagas, like the Icelandic ones, contained more than their share of brutality, violence, and rapscallion antics, delivered in a similarly nonchalant prose. They cut off his head and that was that. . . . I thought these ladies a gang of medieval Icelanders, too.

Human beings must be lonesome on this lonesome planet orbiting through lonesome space, since we seem to want so many relatives to keep us company. Sometimes, a Western Icelander (as they call themselves even to this day) comes into Genealogy Central at the old cooperative store, bringing, from Canada or North Dakota or wherever, the scratched, century-old names on a sheet from an old notebook, to hand them over to whatever genealogist is on duty that day. What's the farm name? What year were they born? (Close is enough, the computer is smart.) In goes the information. The screen glows, the mechanism whirs. "*Augnablik*," the screen reads: literally, "an eye blink," or, "Just a second—hold your horses." Words appear, then numbers. "There are 4,627 listings. Do you want more?" You have just added 4,627 names to your brood. Is the planet getting less lonesome now? If you track down only a hundred of the living, will you have time for coffee with each of them? Will they be pleased to meet you, long-lost cousin? What have you folks been up to for the last century and a half?

There is something touchingly human and comic in this scene, as it plays itself out daily in this little town. Yet as hobbies—even hobby horses—go, genealogy is mostly a sweet and harmless pursuit, a desire to tie your own life and your own body into a larger history.

I once asked Nelson Gerrard, a now-retired high-school English teacher from Arborg, Manitoba, and perhaps the most skilled and knowledgeable genealogist of Icelandic families, "Why? What's the point?" Nelson, himself half Icelandic (his mother, of course), is a careful, soft-spoken, and courteous man. He studied at the University of Iceland when he was young, learned fluent and amazingly correct Icelandic, and indulged his passion for tracking family histories. He's published several books on emigrant history and genealogy, and means to do more when he retires from teaching. Nelson does not take lightly his responsibility to find accurate information for those who ask him. He thinks that for Icelanders (I'd enlarge the generalization to humans, though Nelson is more careful), it's an old instinct, buried deep in Scandinavian and other history—the tribe, the clan, the mutual protection society, the Norse Mafia family. You must take in your kin, feed them, house them, protect them, and avenge them if necessary.

The Icelandic sagas provide plenty of evidence of this mentality. One local example is particularly illuminating. During settlement days a rascal named Hrolleifur arrives in Iceland with his Norwegian witch mother, Ljót (literally, "witch"). He goes to visit Sæmundur, his uncle. Sæmundur is a Hebridean, an original immigrant to Iceland ("land taker" is the Icelandic word), and the chief man in Skagafjörður. *Vatnsdæla Saga* (The Lake Valley Tale) recounts: "Sæmundur said that he could not deny his kinship with Hrolleifur, but I fear that you have a worse mother than father, and I am very much afraid that you take more after her side of the family than your father's.'" Nevertheless, Sæmundur boards mother and son for the winter, then (hoping to be rid of him) acquires a farm for Hrolleifur in an empty valley in north Skagafjörður, far from Sæmundur's own farm. Hrolleifur's uncle advises him to improve his behavior and stay out of quarrels with his neighbors. He doesn't, of course. After wearing out his welcome in Hrolleifsdalur (still named for him after a thousand years), Hrolleifur is shunted into the custody of Ingimundur, Sæmundur's foster brother and the big cheese of the Lake Valley, just to the east. He says to Ingimundur that Hrolleifur is, of course, a villain, and his "disposition does not seem easy to deal with, but he is nevertheless my kinsman. . . . Take him in, along with his mother, and find them a home near where you live." Ingimundur senses disaster but takes Hrolleifur in anyway; he's family. The worst comes to pass: Hrolleifur winds up impaling the elderly and unarmed Ingimundur with a spear in a quarrel over salmon-fishing rights.

Still, Ingimundur's dying wish is to avert revenge. Hrolleif is kin, after all. He's in the ætt, another blip on the family computer. Ingimundur's sons, much to the relief of any reader who is not kin, ignore their father's wishes and, in a fine battle, cut off Hrolleifur's head. It was a head that certainly needed removing. Ljot, the witch mother, tries to save her son with a spell: "She pulled her clothes up over her head and was walking backwards, with her head thrust between her legs. The look in her eyes was hideous—the way she could dart them like a troll."

Hrolleifsdalur is seven or eight miles north of my house. Ljótsstaðir, a farm named for the old witch, is perhaps a mile away in Unadalur (Uni's Valley), just across the road. My friend Valgeir's mother, Didda, was raised on a farm in Hrolleifsdalur. I spent a sunny July afternoon exploring the still-farmed sites named for these ancient rascals. The view north over the sea and mountains from Hrolleif's Valley is sublime in its sweep and grandeur. The sheep looked fat and happy. The river that flows through the valley is underlaid by hot water, which will eventually be piped to Hofsós to heat my house and save me money. Ljótsstaðir is a big working farm, decorated with a lot of old machinery, a garage, great numbers of beautiful horses, and a meadow full of breeding redshanks and plovers. Who knows? Hrolleifur might be in my ætt. Certainly not Ljót! She's the immigrant, the outsider, the conspirator against the integrity of the indigenous culture; she's the Shia, the Sunni, the Jew, the infidel, the atheist, the threat to our way of life. Not our kind. . . . Still, like a good dispassionate student of genealogy, I'm half-grateful to live next to the lovely places still named for these ancient villains. They're kin, part of the clan bound to us by history.

Nelson Gerrard tries to disabuse his clients from entertaining the common notion that Iceland's (or presumably any other) society was ever classless. A genealogy table will demonstrate that chieftains (goðar in Icelandic), the neighborhood leaders and big cheeses, like Sæmundur and Ingimundur, passed down their wealth, their positions, and their eminence for countless generations. Sheriffs begat sheriffs, bishops begat bishops, big farmers begat more big landowners. Conversely, slaves, hired hands, kitchen girls—the lumpenproletariat— begat more of their own kind. This is not a hard and fast rule of history, but it is a much-documented pattern. It is pleasant and honorable to think of ourselves as the exception—the descendant of poverty, failure, oppression who rises triumphantly in the world of affairs. Sometimes we do. On the other hand, the genealogist might inform us that we have inherited our advantages, and that may not be such cheerful news.

Iceland offers a genealogist one great advantage: the continual pruning of the population by plague, starvation, and volcanic eruption. The country was settled between 870 and 1100 by a stream of immigrants from Norway, Ireland, Orkney, the Hebrides, etc., finally reaching (in 1100) a population historians estimate at around 50,000 or 60,000. Most of the names—and the farms—of the original settlers were recorded, and after 1100 there was little or no influx. The families—the ætt—were in place. The population rose to 70,000 by the fifteenth century, when two bouts of the plague trimmed it by 60 percent. In 1703, the 50,000 surviving Icelanders were trimmed to 37,000 by smallpox (plus the usual starvation). The population had recovered to 50,000 by 1786, when another outbreak of smallpox and a gigantic volcanic eruption under the big glacier Vatnajökull covered the whole country with drifts of poisonous ash. The ash killed hay fields, sheep, cattle, and horses, and thus a good number of Icelanders. Back down to 39,000. I've read speculations that the dying continued till 1800, leaving perhaps 30,000 Icelanders as the carriers of whatever genes survived. Back went the population to 70,000 by 1870, but poverty, horrible ice-bound summers (hence more starvation), and another mammoth poison-ash-spewing eruption at Askja precipitated the sizable emigration—roughly 20,000 Icelanders—to the New World between 1870–1914. Throw in a good dollop of leprosy and tuberculosis, and you've got the history of my ætt and their passage from the wilds of east Iceland to Minneota. Here I am, still alive. . . .

It's an impressive history of suffering, but not unusual on our kindly planet. Many places were luckier, a few worse off. But one of Iceland's old miseries may resonate with Americans: in 1627, Iceland suffered an Islamic terrorist attack of sorts. Icelanders call it the Turkish attack, though in fact the perpetrators were Algerian and Moroccan pirate raiders—from the old Ottoman Empire. They landed first at Grindavík, captured 15 Icelanders and a few Danes, captured a Danish cargo ship, besieged Bessastaðir (now the seat of the president), landed in the East Fjords, captured 110, killed 9 (surely some of my ætt!), proceeded to the Westman Islands, where they captured 242, killed 40, burned the church and the warehouses, and then escaped to Algeria with their booty and captives, whom they enslaved or killed. Ten years later, 27 were ransomed to Copenhagen, but some had converted to Islam and refused to come home. I like to think that some stray DNA from Iceland has escaped and prospered in an Ottoman ætt—Osama bin Þorgrímsson? Hallbjörn bin Laden? The defenseless Icelanders waited patiently for the returnees and extracted no revenge. One captive girl was impregnated by Séra Hallgrímur Pétursson, Iceland's greatest religious poet, in Copenhagen, and later became his wife. Maybe preemptive marriage works better than other preemptions in the face of terrorist attacks.

In any case, thirty thousand is not much of a breeding pool. I've heard it said that all Icelanders fall into eight clans, and back no more than a few generations they are all related to one another. Most of Nelson's genealogy seekers would, of course, prefer to find their family tree adorned with important ancestors: intellectuals, chieftains, sheriffs, priests, heroes, and, particularly sweet for Icelanders, a great poet or two. One of my American cousins acquired a family genealogy that passed back before the settlement (in 874), to origins among mythical kings of Norway, Denmark, and Britain. This is, of course, genealogy as fantasy—or wish fulfillment—one of its possible wacky directions.

Egil Skallagrímsson is omnipresent in genealogies; he's the greatest Scandinavian poet of the Middle Ages and a fierce, violent fellow. Bishop Guðbrandur Þorláksson of Hólar, who printed the first Icelandic translation of the Bible in 1584, also appears in thousands of ætts. But the preeminent ancestor is Bishop Jón Arason (also of Hólar in the north—there was a southern bishop, too, at Skálholt). He is in my ætt list, and in yours, too, if you've got even a smidgeon of Icelandic blood. He seems to have been, much more than George Washington or Simón Bolívar, father not just of his tribe but of the whole nation. He was the last Catholic bishop (thus theoretically celibate) and died heroically in defense of the faith, along with his considerable property and power, in 1550. Iceland was so far away, so small, that Rome's arms were not long enough to enforce priestly celibacy, or else they simply were not interested. The Icelanders, in religion as in so many other affairs, often went their own direction without much interference from outside authority.

The Reformation arrived in Iceland in the mid-sixteenth century, not as a spiritual reawakening—or even much of a quarrel about theological ideas. It was, as Gunnar Karlsson describes it, "a revolution from above." It was about farms or, to give it a broader context, land: the power to tax, punish, reward, confiscate, and accumulate. At the time Iceland was hardly used to the idea of Christianity itself, and certainly not to Catholicism. The country was first Christianized in 1000 by vote of the Althing (Parliament), under the threat of force from King Olaf of Norway. Give up your pagan ways or my large army arrives with axes raised and bows drawn. Now, five centuries later, Denmark, in order to consolidate the king's legal power and to enrich the royal treasury with the wealth of the monasteries and bishoprics, was threatening to impose Lutheranism on Iceland from above. As is usually the case with religious revivals, there was much plotting, double-crossing, and killing. In 1541 the southern bishopric, Skálholt, fell into the hands of the Danish Lutherans. The king's sheriff arrested the blind old bishop Ögmundur and took him to Copenhagen, where he died shortly. Gunnar Karlsson reports, "His considerable private property—forty-seven farms and hundreds of ells in silver—was confiscated by the crown." Jón Arason, the northern bishop, came south with a large armed force, not only to avenge Ögmundur but also to keep the south safely

Catholic, with its farms and wealth retained for the church—and, of course, for Jón.

By 1549, he was the last Catholic bishop in Scandinavia, and so the Danish king decided to act again. Jón had assumed the southern bishopric at Skálholt for himself. He had also restored the already-sacked monasteries, and is reputed to have announced, "Now the whole of Iceland submits to me, except for one and a half cottar's sons." Spoken like a humble servant of the loving Christ. Jón Arason was no St. Francis.

But the half cottar's son, the sheriff Daði Guðmundsson, proved his undoing. In the summer of 1550, Jón went west with thirty men, including two of his sons, Ari and Björn, to summon Sheriff Daði to a lawsuit. But Daði had assembled a larger militia, and after a fierce, bloody battle, Jón and his sons were captured and taken to Skálholt to await trial the next year in Copenhagen. The southerners were understandably nervous about the possibility of Jón's escape or of an invasion by a yet-larger force of irritated northerners. Then someone suggested (in a famous Icelandic sentence), "The axe and the earth will keep them best." On November 7, 1550, Jón and his sons were beheaded without trial at Skálholt. Jón's daughter Þórunn initiated the revenge in 1551, with a force of sixty that came south, killed Jón's jailer, and wiped out every Danish administrator in the country. The next spring, another of Jón's sons, Sigurður, came south to retrieve his father's and brothers' bones to Hólar, where they remain to this day.

Jón viewed the Reformation in Iceland as a war between Icelanders and Danes for power and wealth, not as a religious struggle. By 1552, the king of Denmark had again sacked and looted all the monasteries and presumably confiscated most of the three hundred and fifty farms once under Jón's control. Iceland was now thoroughly Lutheran, and for several centuries completely supine under the Danish boot.

That story is at the beginning for all of us—the Ur-Ætt. Icelanders revere Jón as their greatest hero—his fight not primarily for God but rather for the independence of Iceland. They admire him not only for his martial exploits and undoubted courage, but also because he was a skilled poet. He's an odd hero, like Egil Skallagrímsson a combination of literary genius and personal savagery.

I asked both Nelson, the genealogist, and Jón Aðalsteinn Baldvinsson, the current bishop of Hólar and a most learned and charming man, the same question. Can it be possible that every Icelander carries about a little of Jón Arason in his or her DNA, or is it simply wishful thinking to be identified with the great man of Icelandic history? Both agreed that, to quote Martin Luther, "It's most certainly true." I think I like having a greedy, ambitious, thoroughly uncelibate Catholic bishop who composed fine poems on his way to do battle with his enemies rattling around in my gene-pile. Jón's skull and his bones presumably rest under a wooden bell tower next to the fine eighteenth-century miniature cathedral in Hjaltadalur—a grand and beautiful valley full of fertile pastures, native birch woods, hot springs, steep and precipitous mountains. The tower was built in 1950, to commemorate the four-hundredth anniversary of Jón's beheading. There are a lot of severed heads buried around Iceland: Grettir's head under a boulder at Bjarg, Egil Skallagrímsson's uncrackable skull in Mosfellsdalur. Maybe that's the real definition of genealogy: the discovery and location of the buried heads in your own life. They may need a bell tower.

One of the great difficulties of compiling a genealogy is that by the time you've decided to do it, everyone who might have been useful to you—identifying pictures, supplying firsthand information—is either dead or senile. The melancholy quotient rears its head again—forever. You're on your own, with only a few frail strands of evidence with which to reconstruct your own unraveled history.

All my grandparents were dead—some very long dead— by the time I arrived. You have already met my grandmother Kristín from Þingeyjarsýsla, who died in 1933, and Grandpa Herman, who died in 1942. My father's father, Sveinn Holm, died in 1909 of pneumonia, leaving his widow, Ingibjörg Björnsdóttir Gíslason Holm, to raise their five children. She lasted to within a month of meeting me—July, 1943. All those heads are buried not in Iceland, but in Minneota.

My grandmother Ingibjörg (always called Emma) presents particularly thorny problems for any genealogist, even the skilled Nelson. She was born in 1873 on a farm in Vesturárdalur, in Vopnafjörður, in east Iceland. She is listed in Icelandic emigration roles as being six years old in 1879, and a *bóndadóttir*— the farmer's (Björn's) daughter. Her six siblings are listed only as *born*, the farmer's children, with Aðalbjörg, his third wife. Ingibjörg's mother is not listed. One of her "brothers" was also born in 1873. Was she a foster child? A half-Gíslason? Old Björn seems to have fathered children by five women. My Auntie Ole always referred to her grandfather—not affectionately—as Old Bjossi the Fence Jumper. It was always assumed among the Minneota descendants that the Holms were half-Gíslasons— for whatever glory that amounted to. But who was on the other side of the fence when he jumped? I didn't ask such questions when I was a boy.

Who was my great-grandmother? I got a partial answer from my three Holm aunts (Soffia, Olympia, and Dora), and from a Gíslason cousin, Olive, who is the family genealogist. Emma's mother, Sigríður Sigfúsdóttir, lived with Emma (and her many children) in her little widow's cottage on the northwest edge of Minneota. My aunts, of course, remembered her, but I asked them no questions either. I found her marker in the Icelandic graveyard in Minneota. The Gíslason clan is buried in yet another graveyard, where I am myself a small landowner. The stone reads: SIGRÍÐUR SIGFÚSDÓTTIR 1840–1924. The grass had not been cleaned away from the headstone for a long time when I found it, fifty-odd years after her death.

Many years ago I wrote a book of biographical essays about the Icelandic emigrants to Minneota and the surrounding districts. In one of the essays, I reprinted and meditated on old photographs, mostly family. Helga Brogger, my mother's friend and 1929 classmate, gave me a photograph that looked to be a century or so old. Its subject was simple: an old Icelandic lady sitting on a porch and spinning wool, wool that was probably sheared from sheep raised in Westerheim Township by immigrant farmers who still hadn't learned that real money came only from row crops, hogs, and cattle. The treeless prairies stretch off mistily on the right side of the picture. Her barrel waits patiently for rain to come down the spout. She leans forward on her wood rocker, the plaid ruffle on the cushions spread out under her black old-lady dress and gingham apron. A big black bonnet is tied securely under her chin; only a few white wisps of hair escape it. From her dress, wrinkles, and shrunken mouth, we can tell she was no spring chicken when she left Múlasýsla twenty-odd years ago. Her spinning wheel probably traveled across the Atlantic in a wooden chest. It shows no signs of wearing out yet—good for another century, four more generations of yarn. Her black shoe works the treadle; her gnarled hands string the wool strands onto the spindle. From the shadows cast by spinning wheel and barrel, we can see that this was a sunny day, maybe the first fine day of spring—no snow visible on the prairie. I'll bet even money that this old lady would not answer your questions in English. That porch was still Iceland to her, the location changed several thousand miles south and west, but wool still wool, sun still sun. She is the great-grandmother of us all.

I found that picture wonderfully clear and beautifully composed, but Helga had no idea who the woman was and thought it unlikely anyone else would either. The old woman spinning seemed to me an immigrant archetype, a fine symbol of disappeared history in America—the "unknown Icelander."

Then a year or so after the book appeared, in 1996, I received a letter from Twin Valley, Minnesota, from a lady named Sophia Anderson Monson. With perfect Parker-method penmanship and in meticulous sentences, Sophia informed me that she had discovered my book and, as a long-ago Minneota native, was reading it with interest. She was born in 1903, and she first inquired whether I was the Billy Holm who was confirmed with her sister Olga in 1918. She wrote to me in 1996. Her memory, like her handwriting, was both precise and intact. She had left Minneota just after 1920. I wrote back to give her the news that Billy Holm had married Jonina Josephson in 1932, that both were dead, and that I was Little Bill, their son. She wrote back a few weeks later, sent photographs of my aunts and my father taken in 1912, and another of my father and two of his buddies from 1915 or '16.

But there was another surprise for me, even a shock. Sophia's family, the Norwegian Andersons, lived next door to my grandmother Emma's little house. The Holm children were her childhood playmates and friends. And Sophia knew very well who the old lady on the porch was. She informed me that the unknown Icelander was Sigríður, my grandmother's mother, photographed on my grandmother's porch, around the time of World War I. She was a very sweet old lady, said Sophia, but she never said a word in English. Sophia spoke to her in Norwegian. Why do you refuse to identify or claim your own great-grandmother? she sensibly asked. Ignorance, Sophia—I hope not hardness of heart.

I visited Sophia several times in Twin Valley for coffee, cookies, and unimaginable stories about Minneota before World War I, recounted with her perfect memory and sense of detail. She lived alone in her apartment till almost her hundredth birthday, when bad eyesight moved her to her daughter's house in Fargo. She presented me with a particular treasure, a delicate porcelain coffee cup from my grandmother's cupboard. Emma served guests in these, her best dishes. Sometimes the Gíslasons (her half-brother's wives) would come for coffee, Sophia remembered. Presumably Emma brought out the good cups, but Sigríður was always forced to remain out of sight upstairs. The Gíslasons did not want her visible under their noses.

What good is the coffee cup? Sophia kept it for seventy or eighty years because she remembered with affection the woman who drank from it. She passed the cup—and the story—on to me, though I had never met Emma. I will keep it too, and Marcy will likely keep it for a while after Sophia and I have disappeared. But eventually someone will pick up this slightly chipped, discolored coffee cup, look at it briefly, say the hell with it, and chuck it into the nearest dumpster. Genealogy is a melancholy science, but, like the old Zen masters, we continue pursuing it to thicken the plot.

Every pecking order, like every well, has a bottom. In Iceland, in the nineteenth century—and for many centuries before—the *vinnumaður* and the *vinnukona* occupied that bottom. The literal English equivalent is simply "workman" and "workwoman"— hired hands on a farm, landless, positionless, penniless. They filled the back rooms on the manor farms and did the grunt labor of household, field, and barn. Their station and status on the farm were slightly superior to domestic animals—or maybe not, depending on the quality and price of the animals. They were assigned (or rather bound) to their farms by a legal code and its instrument, the local sheriff. They had no right to travel or to improve their positions by moving elsewhere. Nor, as paupers, could they marry and thus legally reproduce. Being humans, they bred anyway, of course, creating the next generation of bottom dwellers. This legal and economic system may not have been the equivalent of slavery in the United States, but it was close. The Icelanders were merely paler versions—probably dirtier and sicker, being less well nourished and confined to smaller living spaces in this cold, inhospitable place—than their African cotton-picking brethren in Mississippi.

This system prevailed in most of Scandinavia, with the sheriff's authority supported and defended by the local state Lutheran clergy, who encouraged piety, submission, obedience, hard labor, and thinking on the soon-to-arrive joys of the next world. A character in the Swede Vilhelm Moberg's novel *The Emigrants*, the half-retarded and illiterate Arvid, hears a description of slavery read to him by his friend Robert. Arvid says that when he emigrates, he plans to become a slave. Robert tries to explain why this is an impossible ambition. But, says Arvid, your book says that a Negro slave can have his own little vegetable garden and own his own pig—and I could never have those things in Sweden. Nor in Iceland.

I am the descendant of a long line of vinnukonur, on both sides. How's that for a distinguished genealogy? You have already met my grandmother Kristín, a vinnukona on a big farm when she left for Canada. Had she remained in Iceland, my grandmother Emma was probably doomed to the same fate. Her mother Sigríður was herself a vinnukona and a descendant of one. In fact, with the exception of a Jewish merchant in the sixteenth century (Jews were forbidden to practice business in Denmark itself, but were welcome to the dregs of their empire: Iceland, the Faroes, Norway, and Greenland), it's vinnukonur (and vinnumenn) all the way down my genealogical table—until, of course, you arrive at the distinguished Jón Arason. At least a vinnukona or vinnumaður was paid for her or his labor: a pittance, or more probably a stingy version of board and bed. There was even a possible rung down the social ladder—to *niðursetningur*, a "set down pauper," those legally barred from labor because they were old, sick, drunk, crippled, or retarded.

What can we know of old Sigríður at the distance of a century and a half? She is listed in the emigration roster as a vinnukona at Búastaðir, another farm in Vopnafjörður—the second farm from Björn Gíslason's farm, Haukstaðir. She left in 1879, the same year as the Gíslasons, also aboard the *Çamoens*, the Scottish steamer that carried Icelandic horses and emigrants first to Scotland and then to England for the second half of their journey to Quebec, and finally on to Minneota.

And who is Sigfús, her father? The trail is faint, but Nelson's acute investigative skills helped track him down in the records. Sigfús Sigfússon was the father of three children outside his marriage, all by different mothers. Another fence jumper, though of lower status? Sigfús was a vinnumaður before his marriage in 1845 to Dagbjartur, after which he became a smallholder at Sunnudalur. Did he marry the farm? His two extra daughters, Ölveig and Sigríður, were born in 1837 and 1838 to different mothers, and son Árni in 1849 to Ölveig's mother—this *after* Sigfús's marriage to Dagbjartur. Daytime television in Vopnafjörður a century before electricity arrived! Sigríður is listed as forty-two years old in 1879, not thirty-nine as her American tombstone would have it. She was thirty-five or thirty-six when her daughter Emma was born. Árni Sigfússon, the half brother, was younger. Árni emigrated in 1873 from Ljótsstaðir in Vopnafjörður, though not to Minneota. He was a *Brasilíu-fari*, part of a small group that left north Iceland for Curityba, a city in the south Brazilian highlands. It was cool, fertile, and lovely, judging by descriptions and photographs; certainly the best destination of any the Icelandic emigrants chose. You could grow your own coffee there—along with a multitude of fruits, vegetables, and grains the Icelanders had never seen or heard of. The foul, chicory-loaded coffee sold by the Danish *factors* was a prime irritant and impetus to emigrate. Scandinavians took coffee seriously then, as they still do.

Árni Sigfússon discovered in Curityba that Brazilian neighbors found Icelandic names unpronounceable. Sigfús, Árni's father, was the smallholder on the farm Sunnudalur in the side valley of the same name in Vopnafjörður, so he took as his Brazilian name Söndal, which is easier to get your tongue around. Fierce Icelandic consonants gave me my Swedish last name, too. As Icelanders understand so well to this day, family names are always negotiable; it's the first name—what you are called while you are alive—that counts. Family names seem designed only to provide not-always-reliable clues for Nelson and his genealogist comrades. The Jews recognize only matrilineal descent; your mother is always and only your mother, but you can never be absolutely certain about Dad. Who knows what Mom was up to? I think Icelanders share this inclination to trust Mother.

So far, that's the best I can do at tracking Emma Holm's line backward. The Gíslason line—should Old Bjossi be the father—is easier. He was a *hreppstjóri* (township commissioner) and married into his first large farm, Grímsstaðir, so the family chart jogs along easily back to Jón Arason, where we all meet. What have I actually discovered about Emma, my grandmother who barely missed my arrival in 1943? I own pictures of her, both as a lovely, soft-faced young woman, then as an old, plump, saggy-breasted, kindly looking, white-haired lady in baggy dresses and black shoes with her socks rolled up. In a picture from her 1893 wedding to the dashing-looking twenty-seven-year-old Sveinn Holm, she is resplendent in an Icelandic *búningur,* with a long white train and a garland of flowers in her hair. She rests her hand on the seated Sveinn's shoulder. She is twenty. Life has unpleasant surprises in store for her. Her five children arrived between 1896 and 1906; my father, Bill, was her youngest. She began her long widowhood in 1909 in the little cottage next to Sophia's family. Even then, housing in Minneota (a miniscule village) was segregated by religion and ethnicity. The blocks around St. Paul's Icelandic Church were called "Little Reykjavík" (though most of the Icelanders had never been to the "big" one). The Norwegians clustered around their church south of the railroad tracks, and the Catholics, mostly Irish and Belgians, on the northwest side. Emma and her children settled among the Catholics, close to St. Edward's Church—as did Sophia's family, the Andersons. Who ever thought the herd instinct didn't operate in humans as it does in codfish and lemmings? I'm pleased to descend from outsiders.

I also own a watch fob woven from her long chestnut hair, an old custom. A small opal is set in the brass fitting. And, of course, I own one of her "good" coffee cups. It's quite enough of a patrimony.

Emma left a fine photograph of her own mother, Sigríður—the lowly. She's dressed in formal black (it's a shoulders-and-up portrait), with a thin, fine-boned, aristocratic face; large, clear eyes; a calm yet melancholy mouth, and a firm chin. Her white hair is pulled tightly back, probably into a bun, like a dancer's hair. She has a long, shapely neck (the Redgrave sisters share it) and a simple oval brooch at her throat. If her name hadn't been clearly written on the back, I'd have thought her the lady of the manor, an Icelandic countess. She was probably around seventy when the picture was taken. She lived a long life—till eighty-seven, if the immigration records are correct. And she still looked alert ten or fifteen years later at her spinning wheel!

Emma spent her life, as the memories of her grandchildren and neighbors testify, caring for and feeding children—and not only her own. As Auntie Dora said to me, "Ma loved everybody up." She worked as a housekeeper and nanny, a vinnukona, for her Gíslason relatives. One of the children from a family she worked for said that she loved Emma as her own mother, rather than her chilly and imperious stepmother. When he died in 1909, Sveinn left her their 280-acre farm in Swede Prairie Township. Two of her half brothers had started a business in land speculation after World War I, so Emma gave them responsibility for managing her property. Students of economic history know what happened next. The Globe Land and Loan Company (and the thousand other such speculative entities) collapsed into bankruptcy, and Emma and Sigríður found themselves as broke as they would have been in Iceland. My father spent fifteen flinty years trying to buy back his own father's farm in Swede Prairie Township. So much for getting rich in the New World. He finally succeeded in 1943, the year his only son arrived. He had help from World War II. Convulsions of human violence keep farm prices high and markets hungry.

As Sigríður boarded with her own daughter till her death in 1924, so Emma boarded a good deal of the time with her own daughters until her death in 1943. My older cousins always interrupted their affectionate stories about her with, "But you don't remember her, do you, Billy?" Indeed I didn't, but I loved the stories. There was no excitement at all in them. They always involved feeding: thin pancakes, *kleinur* (crooked doughnuts), brown bread, *kæfa* (head cheese or jellied meat), *lifrarpylsa* (liver sausage with suet and onions boiled in sheep's intestines), and always coffee (with no chicory), then being hummed into calm sleep. Emma seems to have been the vinnukona-grandmother of everybody. Not a bad fate and vocation for the culmination of a long line of vinnukonur. Jón Arason couldn't have done better himself.

Genealogy—the melancholy quotient—offers those who pursue it with care, intelligence, and no wishful thinking both a wedge into one's personal history and the connection of that history to the larger history of human beings on the planet. It should make us smarter, more humane, and more suspicious of authority, political schemes, and violence of any kind. But above all, genealogy casts a skeptical light on those who claim to have corralled truth. There is no such thing as absolute truth, as you discover if you muddle around in the history of the poor—of vinnukonur, niðursetningur, and whatever depths you might find in your own family. One more fact will always turn up just when you least expect it, overturning all your presumed certainties.

The view out the windows of Brimnes as I write these lines is not good. The weather has been terrible all summer, and for me, as a confessed claustrophobic, the worst kind of terrible. A pale gray to almost white scrim of fog and mist has fallen over the whole fjord and hangs for days, weeks, now months. No mountains, no sky, no clouds. What little you see of the water is the same pale color as the absent sky. No meadows, only damp, gray grass, and the cold mist. All color has blanched to what a house painter would call off-white. As an American, I think of Melville's "The Whiteness of the Whale" from *Moby Dick*, the most eerily terrifying description of any natural phenomenon I know in literature; or the end of Poe's *The Narrative of Arthur Gordon Pym of Nantucket*, with its lost ship disappearing in a milky white cataract.

But in looking west, I have in mind a fog not merely natural. This fog is of the soul and not of the weather report—or, if you dislike "soul," then of history, genealogy, human affairs. For as I look into the blank, endless whiteness, it seems to me that the deepest lack of visibility lies not in the eight miles of invisible fjord leading to Tindastóll, but rather across the Atlantic. The fog travels over the Denmark Strait, the Greenland ice, the vast Canadian forest, and covers the whole of the United States—my house, my job, my ætt, history, political life, and indeed, consciousness itself. I find myself in a state of confused fog that only deepens as I age, the more I see around me.

Part of the passion for genealogy, the uncovering of ancestors, comes, at its most intelligent end, from a desire to slice through this fog. To clarify the soul. The scientist who examines the history and evolution of bones, cells, organisms, continents, and galaxies is only slicing through fog and trying to clarify from another end. Bach in *The Art of Fugue* (and countless other places in his work) slices through the fog at the bottom of the half-dozen notes he explores, to clarify them, to see what beauty, harmony, intelligence, wisdom, and history lies beneath them. Bach made music of his solution, which is surely the most attractive and maybe the truest and wisest of all paths through the fog. But all these paths converge if we follow them with enough energy. Like your genealogical table, they will never arrive at certainty. Their job is rather to move on, or, to summon the Zen masters again, to thicken the plot.

That's what I saw and felt in the melancholy quotient my cousin Bill wished on me—a consciousness of my own death, of the disappearance of everything I've loved or done, and also of the extent of my failure and stupidity. If those people are dead, so will I be soon. This is not a new subject for literature, but it is probably, at bottom, the only one. How right Wallace Stevens was that "Death is the mother of beauty." And of wisdom, too, for that matter. Yet with what delight I discover that some forty-seventh cousin of mine in Curityba is named Zarathustra Magnusson Söndal, born a century ago in 1906, the same year as my father, but handsome as a Latin matinee idol, dark skinned, strong jawed, curly headed, speaking elegant Portuguese, probably fewer than a hundred words of ungrammatical Icelandic (soon to disappear in the mouths of his own children), sitting in a wicker chair in a winter garden, under palms, eating a ripe mango and thinking long thoughts, maybe of his grandfather's and father's Iceland. And perhaps even of some hypothetical forty-seventh cousin from Minneota, Minnesota, most of a century hence, staring out a window in North Iceland at milky fog and thinking long thoughts himself. Of such threads is humanity woven together.

Perhaps not surprisingly, Nelson, the genealogist, is really an artist in disguise. His great passion is for the history of photography. He collects emigrants' old photographs—the work of sixteen turn-of-the-century photographers who opened studios wherever emigrants settled in Canada or the United States. (He hasn't been to Brazil yet.) Many of the emigrants even spent a little of their precious money to be photographed in Iceland. Nelson has collected hundreds (even thousands) of these tintypes, daguerreotypes, and brown-tone cabinet photographs. Many, though not all, are certainly photographic art of high quality, but even the everyday ones preserve faces of great interest, and together they create a remarkable portrait of a culture. Taken together, these pictures form a very large melancholy quotient.

With great taste and intelligence, Nelson assembled an exhibit of these pictures. He calls it "Silent Flashes," borrowing a phrase from a poem by Jón Runólfsson, one of the many skilled immigrant poets. It includes a reconstruction of the Winnipeg photographer Jón Blöndal's studio, along with an eerie life-sized mannequin of Jón ready to press the bulb of the waiting camera. The exhibit opened in Frændgarður (Garden of Friends), one of the old black houses built at the Emigration Center. Half the building consists of an exhibit hall, the other half houses the library and the work center where people come to track their histories. Computers whirr, mice scurry, pages are clipped. The two halves of the melancholy science live together here in the Garden of Friends (it sounds less grand and sentimental in Icelandic).

I often go to Frændgarður in the afternoon for coffee and amusement, to watch the parade of ættfræði seekers huddled around books or a computer, counting new relatives, then going a few feet away to the "Silent Flashes" exhibit to see, if not exactly their family's faces, some similar group. Some find actual relatives; my great-grandfather Jóhannes Sveinsson Holm lives there, and Frida Gilbertson (Hólmfríður Sturlaugsdottir), the most beautiful woman in Minneota in 1913. I knew her as a very old lady, and she was still beautiful. Most of the visitors have lost so much of their history that they can no longer pronounce their ancestors' names. They are only beginning the long burrow into the heart of the melancholy quotient. I wrote a prose poem describing this scene. Try pronouncing it yourself, my friend, in whatever language suits you.

Silent Flashes

In this room a mausoleum
of emigrant faces, embalmed
in brown tone for over a century.

Try pronouncing their names:
Sumarliði, Hrafnhildur, Sturlaugur, Járnþrúður.

The grandchildren give up,
mumble a few consonants.
These faces, once flesh, sweat
in their itchy suits and whalebone corsets,
No weather like this damp heat
before they boarded their boats west.
Now all flesh gone, names too.
Nothing left but brown images,
lit by silent flashes,
the squeezed bulb in the photographer's hand.
Such mustaches! Such intense pale eyes!
Such piles of Norse hair!
Indriði, Árngrímur, Aðalbjörg, Ragnheiður.

Here's a map with pins where they settled,
that weave a spider web over the whole continent,
Gimli, Muskoka, Shawano, Gardar,
Mozart, Minneota, Markerville, Spanish Fork.
A few here, a few there, never many, never enough
so the neighbors ever
get their tongues around:
Hrolleifur, Hrafnkel, Auðbjörg, Þorgerður.

MINNEOTA: THE EARLY YEARS

I was born around three in the morning on August 25, 1943. The arrival took place at the small Clarkfield Hospital in Yellow Medicine County, western Minnesota, hard by the South Dakota border. Some sixty-three years later, I sit at a wooden table in Arizona, writing these sentences much as a sixty-three-year-old man would have written them in 1943. That hypothetical scribbler would have been born on August 25, 1880, and would now be long dead. I scribble on a legal pad with a cheap dime-store pen. Clearly, I would not be scribbling outdoors on February 8 in Minneota, the first town south of my father's farm and the town I still make my home when I am not elsewhere. So I have traveled sixty-three years and several thousand miles to think about 1943 and the time that has galloped by between then and now.

In 1880, the birth year of Scribbler X, one set of great-grandparents had been in America for only a year; another set arrived in 1885. Then, in 1902, the last grandmother. Unlike me, Scribbler X would have grown up bilingual, and may very well have been covering his notepad with Icelandic sentences.

If we think now of a hypothetical Scribbler Y, who is born somewhere on the planet on August 25, 2007, and will therefore be covering something with language in 2070, we can almost be sure that it will very likely not be in this manner. The technology involved in making pages of text into a book will likely no longer resemble my (or Scribbler X's) hand moving across a sunlit page, though this technology sufficed for thousands of years, even before Gutenberg. Indeed, by that time the book itself may well have become an artifact from a dead culture, an anachronistic throwback. But then I can hardly imagine the progress of the next two-thirds of a century any better than a given sixty-three-year-old could have imagined what my adult life would be like from the perspective of 1943. Some days, the future looks dark and witless, others it looks curious and full of prospects. Only one certainty beckons ever closer though still invisible—like any sane human, I would prefer that certainty to remain invisible a good while yet.

My mother suffered a long and difficult labor to bring me into the world that night. My seventy-nine-year-old cousin Wally, who was sixteen at the time, reports that my father appeared on the morning of the twenty-fifth to announce the new son to his sister, Ole, and her husband, Abner. "Oh god, your father was almost crying. 'Jesus,' he said, 'that was awful for Jona. It hurt. You should have heard her hollering. I could hardly stand it. I'll never make her go through that again!'" And he didn't. Their only child arrived in their late thirties, and they never bred again. But whatever difficulties or pain I caused that August night, they loved and indulged me to a fault. I've had sixty-three years' experience at being spoiled, and I'm almost getting good at it.

Aside from birthing a child, what other amusements did western Minnesota have to offer in August, 1943? *The Great Gildersleeve* and *Casablanca* played at the Joy Theatre in Minneota, Bogey and Ingrid on Tuesday the twenty-fourth. My parents sacrificed seeing one of the great American romantic movies to see me into the world. I'm grateful for it.

World War II was in full flower: eight million of our boys and girls in uniform, slugging it out with Hitler, Tojo, and Mussolini. It was the stone at the center of daily life all over the vastness of the United States, even in the upper Midwest. The Iraq War, in contrast, seems hardly to affect daily life in America, other than that of the dead or maimed gladiators and their relatives, all of whom feel the sting of misery and the destruction of war acutely. But the August 25, 1943 weekly edition of the *Minneota Mascot* carried a "Letters Home" column from our boys in uniform. My neighbor Marc Wigness, now eighty, wrote from his boot camp in Idaho that things were going "pretty good." He was then seventeen, on his way to the Aleutian Islands. Buysse Motors offered a few "hard-to-get used cars," among them a '39 Plymouth and a '40 Dodge. A few used tires even showed up in the ads. The quarter-page official civil defense "Air Raid Warning Schedule" proclaimed, "After a two-minute blast, black out house lights, street lights, car lights, and take immediate shelter." This in spite of the fact that Minneota was the snug belly of the continent, far from the theaters of air war.

War bond sales were brisk, with large ads encouraging citizens to invest even more—support the war effort. Prices were modest, but groceries seemed available: coffee cost 29¢ a pound, raisins 14¢ for 15 ounces, Post Toasties 8¢ for a large box, macaroni 5 pounds for 37¢, fresh-made ring bologna just 25¢ a pound at Red Owl, and even scarce sugar, 69¢ for 10 pounds. The editorial for the week of August 25 warned against "Little Things that Make Big Black Markets." All citizens were legally entitled to ration coupons for meat and gas, among a host of other things. But farmers who had their own private meat supplies and legal access to gas for machinery to grow food for the war effort had evidently been sharing their unused ration coupons with friends, relatives, and townies. The *Mascot* reminded readers how unpatriotic such hoarding behavior was— hogging resources that were needed for the war effort—even in little Minneota. I wonder how long our current wars would last if citizens were subject to such a colossal barrage of sacrifice, warning, and finger wagging.

The most peculiar news of the night of August 24 was to be found in a front-page story: "Surprise Blackout Tuesday Evening".

> A surprise blackout, that had been signaled [sic] at about 10:30 Tuesday evening. It met with the usual success in Minneota, with 97 percent of the population falling all over themselves to get under cover, and the other 3 percent out of town, or fast asleep and likewise indifferent to blazing store lights, basement bulbs, and other glaring infractions of the rules.

Could the next accident be your fault?

This the first and only surprise blackout in Minnesota was implemented statewide. Compliance was spotty, judging from contemporary civil defense reports. "Street lights were left aglow throughout the blackout period in Eveleth, Tuesday night. . . . They clearly outlined the entire city to any enemy bombers that might have been overhead." Fortunately, the Luftwaffe hadn't found Eveleth, or, for that matter, Minneota. In Sturgeon, St. James, and even Minneapolis, the blackout was deemed a "total failure." But in Ortonville, a short way north of Minneota, Gus Kleinschmidt, the chief civil defense warden, practiced strict and patriotic diligence.

> Ortonville's chief warden, Gus Kleinschmidt, was similarly incensed after reading an account of seemingly lax enforcement in Minneapolis. In Ortonville we don't monkey around with those who think they are the privileged sons and daughters of some one important. We hauled up before the judge three of our most prominent

merchants, one who particularly told me the night of the Blackout that in as much as his light was very tiny he didn't have to blot it out. He found out differently the next morning. I'll bet you that if ever the next Blackout comes along, test or otherwise, we will have a one hundred percent Blackout, what do you think?

Do you detect a little sarcasm in the *Mascot*'s report of the "usual success"? Do you smell a whiff of the officious petty bureaucrat given small powers, but ferocious self-importance? Might these ghosts of 1943 rattle about under the guise of the Patriot Act?

Meanwhile, as the blackout continued, Jona Holm must have announced to her husband, Bill, that it was time to drive the fourteen miles north to Clarkfield Hospital. The blackout was not a problem for my father's Swede Prairie farm because Rural Electrification wouldn't arrive for another half-dozen years. Presumably the wind generator rested for the night. But Hermann Göring and his ace pilots could have found the headlights on Bill's pre-war Plymouth as it sped north on the gravel roads. I suspect that M. I. Hauge, the elderly Norwegian doctor who delivered me (and half of the county), turned on the electric lights in the delivery room (probably the same room they performed surgery and office duties alike). And at around three o'clock in the morning, I arrived, blackout or no. In the next issue of the *Mascot*, I received my first mention in print: "Mr. and Mrs. William Holm had a baby boy born August 25." Still no name, but nonetheless present and accounted for on the planet.

What other momentous events occurred that day and that year? In New York, the young genius Leonard Bernstein was appointed assistant conductor to Bruno Walter of the New York

Philharmonic on August 25, Bernstein's twenty-fifth birthday. He shortly made his conducting debut in Mahler, and to
universal acclaim. Two years later, he was named Director of
the New York City Symphony, again on his birthday. Now he
really was a made man. Bernstein (like Bach, and maybe like
me) had a sort of superstitious regard for numerology, a sense
that numerical coincidences were not always entirely coin-
cidental. At any rate, I'm happy to share a birthday with one
of the greatest figures in the history of American music. And
with George Wallace. And Carol Burnett. And King Ludwig
the Mad of Bavaria. And Sean Connery. So much for astrol-
ogy. It's a great deal more inexact than numerology. But my favorite sign of celestial benevolence in 1943 was the minting of
the only gray penny in your album. All the copper had gone to
the war effort, so the '43 penny was made first from steel, then
from casings of discarded shells. We '43s can tell with a single
glance at a penny collection when we were born.

But larger numerological coincidences than these haunt
American history. James Carroll—like me, a '43 steel-penny
vintage—was born in the same week as the Pentagon, which
opened for business on January 15, 1943. His father, an officer in the Air Force, would rise in the next seven years to
become first a general and then the head of the Defense
Intelligence Agency. As a boy, Carroll scooted up and down
the endless concrete ramps in the vast building while his father worked late. It was the world's largest playhouse. It was
also the world's largest office building until 1974, when it was
displaced by the World Trade Center. The groundbreaking
ceremony for the Pentagon (built against Roosevelt's better
judgment—he thought it created too vast and concentrated
a mass of military bureaucracy outside his power to control)
took place on September 11, 1941. The Pentagon resumed its

position as the world's largest office building on its sixtieth birthday, September 11, 2001. Convergence indeed. I suppose these questions occur with more frequency as we grow older. But I remember thinking hard on them in 1963 and 1983 and 2003. A birthday has only one destination to progress toward, Wordsworth to the contrary.

Needless to say, the subtitle of one of Carroll's finest books, *The Pentagon and the Disastrous Rise of American Power*, is a succinct summary of our country's nadir. Eisenhower's prescient prophecies of the dangers of the rise of the "military-industrial complex" have exceeded his worst imaginings. We are, as Americans, firmly under the thumb of a monster we ourselves invented. War after war after war after war, the economy afloat on a sea of plunder, the streets deep in blood. And this not to mention the fact that 1943 was also the birth year of the Manhattan Project, which produced the atomic bombs that would fall on Hiroshima and Nagasaki to end World War II, and maybe ultimately to end all of us, present and future. Melodrama, hysteria, naïveté, you say? Read the newspapers (if any journalists are still working) or watch the TV if you own one; I don't and am thankful not to.

But what has any of this to do with Bill Holm, born August 25 at the Clarkfield Hospital during a sudden blackout? Everything! This has been my adult life as an American, with most of it passed in the endless, boring flat of the Midwest. A good number of years have elapsed since Big Bill Holm kept the lights on in his Plymouth in defiance of constituted authority. But what sort of country, culture, and corner of civilization did Bill and Jona bring me home to in Swede Prairie? He was a rough, profane man on the outside, but a tenderhearted elf-child under his striped overalls. At the thought of the blackout or any foolish civil defense warden who might have tried to

stop him, he likely would have said, "Jesus Christ! Goddamn
Adolph Hitler isn't smart enough to find Swede Prairie with
a flashlight up his ass. I'm leaving." And he would have. He
could have been a secret human weapon against the idiocy of
Homeland Security and the Patriot Act, but he has long since
departed this theater of action. He did his part, by his own
lights. And now the question is: How best to do ours?

I am an American—not a proud American, but an American
nonetheless. Neither Jona and Bill nor my grandparents a
generation before them consulted me in the matter. How
can I be proud of a fact about which I had no choice and
for which I took no responsibility? It's only a detail, a statistic, a fact without consequence. Nor did they consult me
about whether I preferred the climate and culture of western
Minnesota. I might have expressed a different preference, had
I been sentient.

But here I am, a card-carrying, taxpaying, passport-holding
citizen, even a continuing resident of western Minnesota. We
only imagine that infinite choice is open to us on our trip
through time to the last reckoning. Our inherited cells, our
DNA, contain the codes for our own death, unless war or accident interrupts them. What we make of all this is, however,
our business—our choice, mostly.

Growing up in Minneota, a number of experiences shaped
my perception of America. Television did not arrive to farms
north of Minneota nor even much of Minneota itself until I left
in 1961. On the farm, we listened to the radio: Cedric Adams
and the news, *Maynard Speece's Farm Hour*, the livestock and
futures prices, *The FBI in Peace and War*, *Whoopee John Polka
Tunes*, Yankton country twang, and, best of all, *The Texaco
Saturday Opera of the Air*, with stentorian Milton Cross and
the hopelessly nerdy intermission "Opera Quiz." I lived for

it—an incipient nerd myself. But while I listened to them attentively—what else for an only child to do on a farm?—I did not love the news: the reports of slaughter in Korea, the Chinese menace, the Russian ogre, the voices of Hoover and Dulles and Nixon warning us of the enemy within, the lurking dangers. Part of my consciousness was further bruised in the early fifties, when I heard the voices of Senator Joe McCarthy and Roy Cohn weaseling out "Communists" in the Army, the State Department, schools, probably even in the Farmer's Union of Minneota. A naïve, isolated farm boy, and not yet having discovered the piano, I knew nothing of the larger world. But I intuited the sound of evil, indeed of madness, when I heard those voices. My father cursed them all as "goddamn fools," but my dread and disgust came not from parental imitation, I think, but rather from a peculiar intuition that seems to have been programmed into my neurological system—a sensitivity to the timbre of the voices, whatever they happened to be saying. Tailgunner Joe and slimy Roy were not voices I wanted to hear in Swede Prairie Township. If they were that hysterical about Communists, the Communists must have a point or two to make. In fact, those voices led me to the *Communist Manifesto*, which I thought full of useful ideas.

But one idea from the radio news seemed even madder to me than the hunt for Communists: nuclear deterrence, or, to use its astonishing acronym, MAD: mutually assured destruction. The idea seemed to be that two empires armed to the teeth (though we were, of course, the empire of virtue, of freedom) faced each other waiting for someone to press the button first, after which the other party would press another button and between them exterminate all life on the planet—except cockroaches, who are armored to survive this holocaust. I heard in this earnest discussion the voices of the school playground: "Nyah, nyah-nyah-nyah-nyah." MAD indeed. Were there actually literate grownups incapable of perceiving the insanity of this logic? Thus, I suppose, was partly hatched my continuing contempt for leaders, authorities, and experts.

Though television hadn't arrived yet, movies had. *On the Beach* haunts me to this day. Like many awkward Scandinavian boys in a world of too many blonds, I was hopelessly in love with the dark and smoky Ava Gardner. Her last weekend in the country with Gregory Peck gives me the shivers when I think of it: that kiss, the blowing curtains, the drunken quartet singing "Waltzing Matilda." What political necessity demanded that murder of Ava Gardner? This was not only her last fling but also the final weekend for the human race. The last shot of the film shows scuttling leaves in an empty street and a billowing banner announcing, "There is still time, brother. Repent." Is there still time? I'm not sure our human foolishness has decreased at all in the meantime.

Dr. Strangelove, the obverse, comic view of MAD, appeared a few years later. All the American paranoia, from Communists to water fluoridators, become objects of ruthless satire in this film. The evil genius and old Nazi retread Dr. Strangelove (played with eerie brilliance by Peter Sellers) has invented the doomsday device—MAD on automatic pilot. In the last clip, Slim Pickens, the archetypical military cowboy, rides his Pinto nuke toward earth while "Don't Fence Me In" warbles on the sound track. Maybe humor and satire—both black—are the only sane responses to the insane rhetoric of the Cold War. And so was born my view of the Communist menace and the threat of nuclear holocaust in America.

I thought Minneota multicultural as a boy. Even in Swede Prairie, I could hear Icelandic, Flemish, Swedish, German, Norwegian, and, by traveling a few miles, Polish and Czech. In the town itself, the doctor was a French Jew and the chicken sexer at the poultry plant was Japanese. A veritable festival of peaceful and courteous neighbors. Lutherans and Catholics even married one another, but that was often not so peaceful. I read tales of slavery and Jim Crow, but that was in the South, not in courteous, civil Minnesota. I'd never met an Indian, though two reservations were close by, and the site of the Dakota War of 1862 was only an hour-and-a-half drive. But then that happened before any of the citizens of Swede Prairie had ever arrived on the continent. That nasty business was over and done with, after which we homesteaded the land and largely turned Republican. I went to a Swedish Lutheran college in 1961, in a class with perhaps a half-dozen black faces, mostly Africans who arrived after being missionaried. The civil rights movement was in the air. Little Rock had been integrated after a fashion, and in Birmingham buses and lunch counters were about to take a turn for the better and more humane. The fifties lasted a long time in Minnesota.

In high school, I served as the local delegate to a summer "American Legion Boys State" week intended to instruct in the fundamentals of American politics and government. But mostly I played the piano for the Boys State chorus and tried to make friends with the counselors—grown-ups, teachers, and college students, who seemed worldlier than my high-school peers. Boys State turned out to be administered largely by the staff of my Swedish college, though it was located on the University campus in St. Paul. A kindly old man in the athletic department was the director. He remembered my piano playing and offered me a weeklong summer job as a counselor. My chief duty was again to accompany the chorus. Apparently pianists were hard to come by.

Though I was suspicious of the patriotic line, I liked the idea of introducing young people to the notion of how government actually works, and so I went in June. I think I was the only nonathlete, probably the only non-coach among the counselors. But I liked them all for the most part. My favorites were a pair of hockey coaches from the east side of St. Paul, a hockey-crazed neighborhood. They were physically rough-looking fellows—big shoulders, bulging biceps, meaty hands—but they were good joke- and storytellers. I liked their violent sagas of hockey brouhahas: how I got this gold tooth, who inflicted this scar. The skilled choral director, a black man from a city high school, was the other nonathlete, but he was also a good storyteller and an amiable fellow. One night, seven or eight of us decided to go out on the town for a few hours, eat a big steak, and drink a few beers. Ah, the excitement! Drinking beer with the old guys! Our counselees were busy with some public event and wouldn't need our supervision for a few hours.

We drove to a steakhouse north of St. Paul, where we were greeted by the owner, who recognized most of them as well-known local coaches. "Good to see you, boys. I'll get you a table." Then he spotted the choral director. "You can't do that. Get the nigger out of here." A most unjovial silence descended on the scene. I was speechless, in shock. One of the coaches, the burlier, began rocking on his feet and curling his fingers as if he were about to deliver a hammer blow. His eyes burned. Two other coaches flanked him. "Cool it, Sam. We don't want this in the papers. Let's just get the hell out of here. We'll go eat cheeseburgers down at Manning's." And so we headed for the popular University of Minnesota bar, but a sort of spiritual shroud had fallen over the gaiety of the evening. The black conductor tried to buck up the crew: "Don't let it worry you. It happens. There are assholes everywhere."

But weren't all the assholes in the South, below the Mason-Dixon line, or in mean eastern cities? Wasn't the refusal of a table illegal by federal law? I thought then of all the lazy nigger and drunk Indian jokes I'd let slip in one ear and out the other.

Maybe there was an interior asshole inside America, indeed inside every culture, every human being. That interior asshole surfaced at strange, embarrassing times, like Dr. Strangelove's involuntary *Seig Heil* in the midst of cabinet meetings. Where was my own interior asshole? When would it show its pockmarked face? Where is your interior asshole? And that is how a Swede Prairie boy came to consciousness of civil rights in America.

For the duration of my adult life, war has been the central national fact. We must love war, we Americans, because we don't seem to be able to figure out how to stay out of them, or, for that matter, how to end them. The Cold War (with hot flashes) was already in process when I left Minneota for college and graduate school, but it had intensified by the beginnings of Vietnam. It didn't take me long to figure out that I did not wish to sacrifice for this mad adventure. I simply didn't believe the domino theory or most of the other power and scare talk I heard from the government. Then as now, that war seemed pure folly to me.

In 1967, just as I finished my master's degree in English at the University of Kansas, I was summoned to appear for a draft physical. I drove from Lawrence to Minnesota to visit the Yellow Medicine County draft board. Maybe they'd made a mistake? Maybe there was a more warlike Bill Holm somewhere in the rural county? The draft office in the county courthouse was presided over by a white-haired lady with thick glasses on a wire chain; she looked like somebody's Norwegian grandmother.

"Why," I inquired, "am I being summoned, since I am both married and currently pursuing a Ph.D.?"

"The county draft board decided that all master's graduates should serve before continuing their studies."

"How many master's in literature in Yellow Medicine County?"

She held up one finger.

As my mother had always assured me, I was a "special" fellow. Fortunately, the Grandma of Selective Service did allow me to transfer the physical from Minnesota to Kansas, since I now lived there.

Kansas required inductees to ride a special military train to Kansas City. I boarded in Lawrence an hour west. We were delivered to a ramshackle hotel in Kansas City for a short night. I quickly gathered that the hotel served as a full-time whorehouse when it didn't double as a draftees' dorm. Many an entertaining venereal disease returned to the cow towns of western Kansas after that night. Many a farm boy's virginity perished. We were awakened at three o'clock in the morning, fed a greasy breakfast (sausage, bacon, and ham—a rare treat for my orthodox-Jewish law-professor roommate) and bussed *en masse*, some three hundred of us, to the induction center. Johnson needed fodder for the Vietnam cannon, and we were it. I sat next to a none-too-bright eighteen- or nineteen-year-old ranch boy from Colby, Kansas: "I can't wait to get over there and kill me some gooks in 'Nam." I have a feeling his name is now chiseled in black stone on the Wall in Washington.

Imagine, if you will, over three hundred young male bodies, stark naked but for their socks (which we were instructed to wear), marching briskly through the steps of the physical, carrying clipboards with attached wooden pencils. Imagine them a dozen at a time bent over, ordered to "spread those cheeks" while a platoon of plastic-gloved hands inserted themselves on discovery missions. Imagine the three-hundred-pound drill sergeant barking "Next" as they moved inexorably to the chest X-ray, and then on to the eye exam. It was a valuable lesson in humiliation, a good preparation for warfare.

Finally, the blood pressure check, the questionnaire: "Are you gay? Are you crazy? Are you a felon?" Then the sentence of doom or salvation: 1-A or 4-F. My blood pressure was a bit high, maybe 160/100. I was twenty-five, tall, plump, heavy glasses, mustache, clearly no athlete. And I probably smelled of books. The doctor assured me shrewdly: "Your blood pressure is too high. It should be controllable with simple medication. If it goes down for six months, you are eligible for service. I'll classify you 1-Y. You'll have to submit a certificate signed by your doctor every six months in order to monitor your progress. Good luck." So I wouldn't have to die a Canadian or a jailbird after all. My local doctor, a family friend, advised me (given my young age) to be contentedly hypertensive for a few years until Lyndon Johnson's appetite for flesh had been satisfied. He signed regularly until the draft adopted a numbers lottery a year or two later. August 25 was a lucky birthday: number 256, as I recall. My blood pressure descended rapidly after a few helpings of the proper pills. The long and short of it is that I stayed off the Wall.

My hatred of that brainless war did not decline with my escape from service, however. I demonstrated regularly, wrote antiwar poems and essays, and trembled in the presence of Robert Bly's "The Teeth Mother Naked at Last," one of the fiercest poems in American literature. The political life of the country seemed an impacted bowel in 1968, as it does again in 2007. No large voices rose to say no, to take responsibility for doing what they could to end the slaughter. Finally Eugene McCarthy, my own senator from Minnesota, could stand it no more and challenged Lyndon Johnson on the issue of the war. McCarthy was a remarkable man, a farm boy from Watson, a failed priest, a true intellectual, a wit, a fine poet, and thus a man with a rare gift for precise language. I was among the millions who responded, the "Clean for Gene" gang. There was a glint of hope again in America. Truth had been spoken and acted upon.

McCarthy came close to beating Johnson in New Hampshire, an amazingly successful challenge to a powerful incumbent. Oregon went for McCarthy. A movement had begun by the impetus of one brave and honest man. Johnson relinquished his political career and millions cheered. After this victory and clearing of the field, Robert Kennedy decided to enter the race (after long declining to take on Johnson, too dangerous, too risky for a career). The journalists immediately switched allegiance and awarded Kennedy the prize—suddenly he was the voice of the poor, the downtrodden, and the humble. McCarthy was dismissed as a fey aristocrat, the cattleman's son with a St. John's scholarship as opposed to Harvard and the Kennedy power and millions. In the end then, McCarthy turned out to be only the stalking horse for real power in America.

I turned twenty-five in the summer of 1968. The Vietnam War continued to rage, as it would until 1975, by which time almost sixty thousand names had been readied for the Wall. In a hotel in Los Angeles, Sirhan Sirhan shot Robert Kennedy, who had looked like a winner; James Earl Ray shot Martin Luther King, Jr. at a motel in Memphis, and Arthur Bremer shot George Wallace, the racist Alabama governor and presidential candidate, at a political rally. My own generation was gassed and bludgeoned in the streets of Chicago at the Democratic convention. The National Guard opened fire on the students of Kent State, leaving several dead or wounded. It was in this America that I launched my professional life. But then profession is not quite the right word to describe how I have passed my life. Vocation is closer—in the sense that a priest claims to have a vocation. Mine was scribbling small poems whose lines usually didn't travel to the end of the page.

In America, it's a little embarrassing to identify your profession on official forms as "poet." A lawyer who filled out my tax forms one year thoughtlessly listed me as a poet. The IRS, which possesses neither sense of humor nor love of art, responded with an audit. Now I say "schoolteacher," a truth with regard to my salary, if not to my love or craving. In social encounters with strangers, I sometimes joke, "Well, I went into the poetry racket; that's where the money is." After polite chuckles, we have another drink and forget about it.

I have not always been faithful to my vocation. At about forty, I decided I had better see whether there was in fact an audience for what I had to say in the world, so I started writing prose, ordinary sentences for the "common reader," as Virginia Woolf called them. In this sense my experience was opposite to Thomas Hardy, who began his writing life with a long say in prose: thirteen fat novels and four books of tales. At fifty-six, after the witless attacks on *Jude the Obscure*, which he knew to be his greatest novel, he finally gave up prose in disgust at the squeamish stupidity of his audience. He vowed to subsequently write nothing but verse and, before his death at age eighty-eight, wrote a thousand-odd pages of poetry, including an epic-length verse drama. He thought verse offered him the chance to say honestly what was on his mind because so few read it or took it seriously enough to be offended. In a famous barbed comment, he said that if Galileo had described the movement of the Earth around the Sun in verse, the Inquisition would have left him alone. He was probably right. W. H. Auden's gloomy view that poetry "makes nothing happen," that it is only "a mouth," is also probably true.

But in 1968, American poets used their art to try to put a stop to the war. American Writers Against the Vietnam War read at universities all over the country to large, usually grateful audiences. I heard several of those readings, and they increased my sad understanding of my own country. William Stafford, a World War II conscientious objector and lifelong crusader for peace and sanity, was the grandfather of the antiwar movement. In the following poem, he celebrates a place on the Canadian border where nothing happened, no guns were fired, no blood shed:

At the Un-National Monument along the
Canadian Border

This is the field where the battle did not happen,
where the unknown soldier did not die.
This is the field where grass joined hands,
where no monument stands,
and the only heroic thing is the sky.

Birds fly here without any sound,
unfolding their wings across the open.
No people killed—or were killed—on this ground
hallowed by neglect and an air so tame
that people celebrate it by forgetting its name.

David Ignatow, my teacher in Kansas and a drastically under-
rated American poet, asks, "How come nobody is being bombed
today?"

All Quiet

How come nobody is being bombed today?
I want to know, being a citizen
of this country and a family man.
You can't take my fate in your hands,
without informing me.
I can blow up a bomb or crush a skull—
whoever started this peace
without advising me
through a news leak
at which I could have voiced a protest,
running my whole family off a cliff.

And Robert Bly, organizer of those readings and a man of remarkable courage, vigor, and genius, suggests in his ferocious, surreal poem, "The Teeth Mother Naked at Last," that it was ourselves we wanted to bomb.

> It is a desire to eat death,
> To gobble it down,
> To rush on it like a cobra with mouth open.
> It is a desire to take death inside,
> To feel it burning inside, pushing out velvety hairs,
> Like a clothesbrush in the intestines—
>
> That is the thrill that leads the President on to lie. . . .
>
> These lies mean we have a longing to die.
> What is there now to hold us on earth? We long to go.
> It is the longing for someone to come and take us by
>   the hand to where they all are sleeping. . . .

Is it possible that our endless warfare, our endless showers of bombs on Vietnam, Panama, Grenada, Sudan, Iraq, and Afghanistan covers our refusal to look ourselves in the mirror, to show us our history and to give up the lies we use to solder our clanking armor securely around ourselves?

But if poetry can reveal the dark side of our history, it can also explore our connection to nature, to our peculiar place on Earth. The three poets in the past paragraph are equally poets of place: Stafford of the rural plains and small towns of his boyhood in Kansas, Ignatow of the crowded streets and gritty industrial environs of New York, and Bly of the frozen cornfields and lonesome farms of western Minnesota.

I suppose I started writing poetry as soon as I could pick up a pencil and spell words. I fingered the half-calf standard poets in the Minneota Library or in the libraries of my parents' eccentric Icelandic pals and relatives. I loved the jingling noise and terror of Poe, and scribbled endless bad imitations. I read Shakespeare because I knew he was top-of-the-line, the big fellow. I probably intoned his sonnets to the barn cats and my father's Labrador retriever, Peggy. At almost ten, I began issuing my opuses, "The Collected Poems of Wm J. Holm, 1953" in editions of one, carefully printing the poems on unlined paper and then sewing them together with my mother's cast-off thread. I remember making up an epic horror story in rhymed verse in which a big pirate statue my mother had painted in ceramics class comes to life, sharpened sword and all, and begins hewing and slaughtering his enemies. After I discovered musical terminology, I began giving the poems musical directions as titles: "Misterioso," "Mesto," "Largo Lugubre." My adoring mother saved all these first editions in a trunk of Little Bill memorabilia, but trust me, Dear Reader, they shall not see light.

For a big blubbery boy to announce to his flinty and practical Minneota neighbors—farmers, carpenters, truckers, drivers of big Caterpillars and combines—that he intended to pursue poetry and the piano invited humiliation at worst, skeptical bemusement at best. But I was lucky. I grew up among the tail end of the Icelandic immigrant community. The old, even the middle aged like my parents, were still bilingual, even bicultural, whether they were born in the old country or here. The smoke of that ancient culture still drifted off them in odd ways. They even read—particularly the old ones—poetry. Many carried hundreds of lines of poetry in their head. A fat boy unsuited to farming but committed to versifying, however wretched, seemed within the bounds of normality to them,

if not a bit admirable, a sign of at least a few brains. Unlike
Alden Nowlan, a farm boy who became one of Canada's finest
poets, I did not have to hunch over to hide from my father the
page on which I scribbled lest he beat me for it. In fact, I often
read my opus-in-progress to the poor man, in hopes of escap-
ing the·slopping of pigs or the gathering of fieldstones. Surely
poetry was a higher calling than farm chores. Sometimes it
even worked.

It was, in any case, always clear to me that language was
the equipage with which I traveled. It is not to my credit that I
acquired only one of them. What was absent from my first literary efforts was the farm: the grove, pasture, pigs, corn, oats,
and cattle. The sloughs with their ducks, geese, cattails, and
muskrat houses. And the prairie weather: the great blizzards,
black thunderstorms, the shredded remains of local tornadoes.
My head lived in the world of books, of words, even if my body
was trapped atop a small hill in Swede Prairie, smelling pig
shit, breathing oats dust, hearing the cries of pheasants, the
crowing of roosters, and the moaning of mourning doves. To
a large degree, I still live in that rarefied world, unless I make a
conscious effort to leave it.

But it is also true that I never wrote a single sentence worth
hearing twice until I had made my way out of that world. I had,
in fact, to leave that farm for college, marriage, job, failure, and
the whirligig of American life and history, before I could see
anything at all about the world. The paradox was that the farther
away I traveled, to places utterly unlike Swede Prairie and my
father's farm, the more clearly I saw and understood the farm,
the more the wisdom it had to offer revealed itself to me.

I found many angles from which to view the farm: from the
south, the east, cities, the west, Europe, China, and a deck above
Lake Washington in Seattle where I saw it clearest of all. But

all this traveling led, finally, to the place my intuition assured and still assures me is the right angle of vision from which to view my life and my country: facing west out the windows of Brimnes.

SILENCE AND NOISE

Age, ancestors, and bad habits have driven me to blood tests two or three times a year, to examine the progress of my proteins, lipids, triglycerides—whatever might predict whether butter and bacon will finish me off before my appointed time. I take these blood tests in a small town in western Minnesota, in a clinic housed in a half-deserted shopping mall. My most recent visit was on a blustery February morning, fifteen below, a cutting northwest wind. The lab opens at 8:00 A.M., and since I had better things to do later in the day, I arrived at 7:50 to beat the syringe rush. An old couple had bested me, but at least I was number two. I settled into the little waiting area to begin examining the pile of magazines: *Golf Digest, Guideposts, Modern Bride, Good Housekeeping, Teen, People,* and my favorite: *Ladies' Home Journal,* with its monthly column, "Can This Marriage Be Saved?" I've been reading those essays in waiting rooms for forty years and have never yet found one I thought could or ought to be salvaged, but the *Journal* always seems to find that with counseling, tolerance, compromise, and improved insight, marriages are invariably meant to carry on jauntily into senility. I glanced up from the current troubled marriage to see that the waiting room had filled, not with quarreling young couples, but rather with, to use a favorite euphemism, senior citizens—the old. I am past sixty and was clearly the bright-eyed boy in this lineup.

I found it hard to concentrate on the collapsing marriage; the sound system boomed out a pop song, heavy bass, a female singer with a voice halfway between a croon and a whine, "my honey broke my heart," with attendant electric-guitar riffs. For me, Muzak is always the moral equivalent of aural sandpaper, but I noticed among the wrinkled white heads a universal expression of stoic misery. All had ceased paging through the magazines, or, for that matter, making any attempt to talk. The whole gang of us sat in stunned silence, doing our best not to listen. Though I didn't catch anyone at it, I'd guess a half-dozen hearing aids were extinguished.

After a few minutes that seemed like hours, I could stand it no more. "Does the music seem too loud to you?" I boomed out. Nods. "Does anyone like it?" Heads shaking. "I'll ask them to turn it down." A dozen elderly heads looked at me as if I were Joan of Arc, or David about to take on Goliath.

I asked the receptionist in a quiet and polite voice if she could turn the Muzak down a bit since it was disturbing the—what might we call them?—the customers. No. You have no volume control? No. Then how about the off button? This awful music is irritating all of us. No. No off button? It has to be done in Willmar. The off button is eighty miles away? Yes. I'll put the call on my bill. Can't do it. Can't call Willmar? Can't change the Muzak? It's programmed by system-wide computer. The computer thinks twenty old people should be tortured by this noise at eight in the morning at fifteen below? It's to protect confidentiality. Confidentiality? Confidentiality.

This conversation had clearly ended. I returned to my seat and confessed to the little morning assembly that a computer in Willmar had decided they would like this Muzak—at this volume. Stoic nods. Without words these weathered faces spoke: so goes the world, we're used to it. The lab opened, and a voice summoned me to part with a vial or two of blood. When I had done so, I rolled down my sleeves, put on my heavy coat, and left, pleased at least by the noise of the wind banging the stop sign to and fro on its iron post.

This early-morning story, repeated thousands of times across these electrically wired United States, offers some wisdom: perhaps most importantly, though Americans think of themselves as rebellious individualists jealously guarding their personal freedoms, we are in fact a nation of mentally drugged cattle. Tell us not to smoke and we don't; tell us to pile in duct tape and plastic wrap because the terrorists are coming and we empty the shelves at Wal-Mart; phone us at dinnertime to sell us doodads and we buy; play us computer music fortissimo to shut us up in public spaces or drain our powers of reflection and we sit quietly suffering through it. We—not the Germans, the Chinese, or the Arabs—seem to me the most easily bullied people on earth. We are duck soup to lead; ask our leaders.

Further, we have become so conditioned to the sloshing oceans of mostly commercial noise that surrounds our every waking moment—television, radio, our various gizmos for producing private tunes in public spaces—that if it all stopped, leaving nothing but wind and water and the sound of the birds, and leaving us to face real silence and our own inferior company for weeks, days, hours, or even minutes, I feel sure we would panic. Our nerves would overwhelm us. We are, in general, not particularly interesting to ourselves anymore, and we have become, therefore, less interesting companions for one another.

Confidentiality? What might old people talk about in clinic lobbies? Cholesterol, their prostates, their biopsies, surgeries and attendant horrors, their bowels and bladders, maybe even gossip about their children, neighbors, or ministers? Horrors! Put a stop to it with the Dixie Chicks on the Willmar computers! But then on the other hand, neither their health insurance

providers nor their governments show any sign of squeamishness about obtaining information on the same subjects with
or without their active compliance. Maybe the insurance and
civil service functionaries are listening to the same computer-
programmed tunes.

When the World Trade Center went down on September 11,
2001, the school where I teach did not cancel classes, so I went
to work: freshman English and rural literature. I started with
the proposition that we would, of course, not do academic
work, but rather take this chance to talk together as citizens
about the morning's disaster. My students, textbook phlegmatic Midwesterners, are never talkative—and that morning,
most seemed especially unsure of what to say. I didn't blame
them; I wasn't sure of anything myself except a growing interior fear, not so much of terrorists as of what this would do
to the public life of our country. A few boys wanted to "nuke
'em"—whoever "'em" was: Muslims, Arabs, foreigners. We were
suddenly without Communists just when we needed them
most. A few mentioned god, indicating that though he was off
duty at 9:00 A.M., he was still on our side and would punish
our enemies. By 2:00 P.M., most of the students assumed we
were either at war or shortly would be, though they weren't
certain against whom—maybe the whole world.

Their reactions and opinions, though expressed without the
sophisticated arcana of public-policy language, seemed to me
to mirror the confusion, bluster, and posturing of the press and
media at the time. We knew nothing but we went on opin-
ionizing, sometimes with aggressive dogmatism. The words
War, God, and *Homeland* drifted through the public discourse
like poison gas, without adding anything intelligent or useful.
The idea was to plant the interior tapes of these opinions into
the consciousness of Americans, so that when hard thinking

was required of them, they could instead depress some interior play button and recite the automatic-pilot response that seemed to pass for thought. That, after all, is the essence of talk shows and news channels. Implant a key word—*God* and *War* are exemplary—and when the subject hears it, the tape begins running. After a while, you could recite most of these tapes yourself, once the key word thundered in.

By September 13, the students asked to return to regular work, reading Orwell and rewriting essays, reading *O, Pioneers* and Robert Frost and thinking about farms in literature. Three days of television had deadened them. "They run the same footage over and over," they said. "After a while it doesn't seem real anymore. It's like a movie." It looked to them like the digital exploding buildings in the blow-'em-up films, an always popular genre. I hesitated to suggest that they might have turned their televisions off, instead of patiently waiting for the return of more entertaining programming. Maybe keep them off a whole day—or a week, a month, a year, a decade, or even (my real advice) a lifetime. But the off button seemed, as in the clinic, to be mysteriously lodged in some cosmic Willmar where "they" had set the programming and it was not our business to tamper with it.

Was it the silence after the dots dissolve into the blank gray screen they feared? For in that silence you are left to your own private questions about what just happened, even, god forbid, a bit of reflection on what might have brought these events about. No martial music, no stentorian voices with the inside scoop, no panels of experts, no spokesman for the administration, no groupthink, only—how frightening—thinking in silence. What if you arrived at ideas different from the Fox network, or from the press secretary, or from the NPR news staff? Suppose some echoes of Homer, Shakespeare, Tolstoy, Thucydides, or Gibbon moved through your consciousness with their heavy, slow-footed, ancient wisdom—the wisdom of history, of the great wheel of fortune, the rise and fall of empires, the hubris of the powerful, the rage of the powerless.

Goethe was not afraid of silence. In what is perhaps his most famous small poem, "Wandrers Nachtlied," he imagines the silence of Nature—indeed, by implication, of the whole universe—internalized. Even if you butcher German, say the poem to yourself aloud; the beauty of the chiming vowels works with the content to produce the same interior effect in reader and speaker.

Über allen Gipfeln
Ist Ruh,
In allen Wipfeln
Spürest du
Kaum einen Hauch;
Die Vögelein schweigen im Walde.
Warte nur, balde
Ruhest du auch.

Over all the hilltops
is silence
In all the treetops
you hear
hardly a breath;
The little birds become silent in the woods.
Just wait. Soon
you will be silent too.

I don't recommend experiencing this poem to the accompaniment of waiting-room Muzak, but if you must have music, try the settings of the poem by Schubert and Liszt, both of which are introspective, lyrical, and quiet. Best of all, sing them to yourself or make up your own tune. Serenade the tree in your garden, or return to the birds the favor of song. In silence, the poem says, we enter the largeness of the universe, both interior and exterior. To know song—or, for that matter, to recognize noise—we must know silence. This poem encourages us to buy nothing. Is it a poem about death—about dissolution into the great pool of being? Among other things, yes. But keep reading it—memorize it. Think it to yourself in waiting rooms. This poem will always honor your confidentiality.

D. H. Lawrence, a noisy man in life, is the twentieth century's great poet of silence in nature and humans. Here is his small poem "The White Horse":

> The youth walks up to the white horse, to put its
>   halter on
> and the horse looks at him in silence.
> They are so silent, they are in another world.

Where is this world? Is it like our world? Do they have talk shows, sound tracks, and digital programming? How do we reach the white horse for a red alert? How do we reach the youth who has disappeared into the black hole of the horse's eye? Walt Whitman said that the look of the bay mare shamed the silliness out of him. In 2003, we have inflicted a great deal of silliness on ourselves, and we need to spend more silent time in the company of Walt's bay and Lawrence's white horse.

Robert Bly, a half century after Lawrence, watered his horse on a winter night in Minnesota.

Watering the Horse

How strange to think of giving up all ambition!
Suddenly I see with such clear eyes

> The white flake of snow
> That has just fallen in the horse's mane!

Ambition for what? Victory, revenge, money, success, power—all devour the alert, interior silence that lets us truly see the single snowflake in its tiny flickering of life before it melts into the cosmic pool.

I could go on with such moments in our literature—Wordsworth standing on Westminster Bridge at dawn, Marvell in his garden, Emily Dickinson the moment after death—but you get the point. These poems are not opinions but rather descriptions of doors into the self, the inner life that is the only source of true nourishment. The eternal noise that electricity has enabled us to create around ourselves manages primarily to drown out those interior voices, to subvert them with commercial messages, behavior management, political cant, and saber rattling. Goebbels was only the first master to use electric sound to plant lies in the consciousness, to turn the human off buttons on simple decency and fellow feeling. His descendants are legion, and for the most part they are not German. They live among us, and they depend on the fact that inside us lives not only the soul nourished by silence and reflection but also a crazed mob endlessly chanting regurgitated slogans, in love with big amps and constant noise, and terrified of the waiting silence in Goethe's "Nachtlied." In all of us. If we let it happen.

Muzak never rests, it never breathes, the magic fingers never offer even a moment of silence, the elevator speakers hum on long after the elevator has fallen. Real music, however, cannot exist without silence. "Play the rests," your piano teacher told you sternly, and she was right. John Cage, our transcendental philosopher of American music, even composed a famous piece, *4'33"*, entirely of silence, in which the pianist comes to the huge grand with a clock, opens the keyboard, raises the wing, sits quietly with folded hands for four and a half minutes, then closes the piano and bows to receive the applause of the audience. A silly trick, said the Republicans of musicology, and maybe they were right, but Cage had, as usual, a dead-serious point to make about the nature of sound in the universe. The shuffling feet of the audience, the raspy coughs, the crinkling of hard-candy wrappers, buzzing of emergency lights, maybe creaking doors, bird cries, passing traffic—all create their own random music. At least Cage honored silence, which is more than the digital computers of Willmar do, or any Kmart in your neighborhood.

All composers worth their salt use silence. How can we know what music is if we do not know its absence? I'll give examples of two uses of silence by genius; if you are a musician, you will think of others. Almost no piece of Haydn is without sudden and unexpected silence, in which the music comes to a stop as if to allow new and startling harmony to assemble offstage before surprising, even shocking, the listener with its entrance. Players are shocked, too, no matter how many times they hear or practice a piece. Particularly in the piano sonatas they must continue to deceive the listener, as if this strange silence followed by new harmony happened under their fingers for the first time every time. What Pound said of literature can also be said of music: that it is "news that stays news." Or of Flannery O'Connor's famous confession that when Manly Pointer stole Hulga the philosopher's wooden leg in the hay barn, in her story "Good Country People," it shocked the author as she imagined and composed it, and it is intended to go on giving readers a shock whenever it happens. Haydn, like O'Connor, must have felt particular pleasure in the furious but often interrupted Presto finale of his last sonata, Sonata no. 52 in E-flat Major. The footnote in my old edition reads, at this interruption, "A considerable pause should be made after the hold itself." A few pages later, the frenzied tempo slows abruptly for the Adagio. The texture thins to a chromatic scale that descends slowly in single notes. Another ample pause. Silence. Then the hammered, speedy rondo theme resumes with renewed energy. These silences are continual surprises for the ear, correctives of a sort for a consciousness that expects patterns to continue ad infinitum. Haydn clearly liked alert listeners—and players. He did not mean for us to sleep through our lives. Some musicologists call these little, slow interruptions collapsing to long silence "fainting spells." These interjections of energy inside any great work of art provide bracing smelling salts for the soul.

Do not try playing Haydn as background music for dinner guests. His sudden surprises will cause indigestion, hiccups, truncated chitchat. Let your guests eat and drink in silence until some witty sentence or fine story interrupts the smacking of lips and clattering of knives and forks. Play Haydn for them after dinner, when they can listen. And play it on a piano if you can, but on a machine if the unkindness of the universe has reduced you to that.

Haydn's fellow descendant of Austrian farmers, Anton Bruckner, is another great composer of silence. Bruckner's huge symphonies, like barges made of obsidian or bronze, float with majestic slowness through oceans of air. They require flotillas of Wagner tubas, trombones, horns, trumpets, winds, and strings in vast masses, underlaid by a thundering of timpani. Bruckner does not write music for gazelles or butterflies, but rather for mountains dancing. They move with the slow inexorableness of glaciers and, when icebergs fall, the listener has been aurally prepared for the great crashing into the sea. Bruckner crescendos take ten or fifteen minutes as the vast orchestra gradually increases in sound, section after section playing to add to the mass. In music *Tutti* means "all together," and when that happens in a Bruckner symphony, the listener feels a sense of drowning in the size and weight of the sound, an aural climax of such beauty, intensity, and size that it stiffens the spine and steals the breath. And then, at the very moment when you cannot imagine that this behemoth could stop before bursting out the walls and roof of whatever hall is trying to hold it, it stops. Just stops. The air resonates for a brief moment longer, and then, silence. The music rests. No tinkling, no single strings, no lonesome oboe. Nothing. Silence. The cosmos taking a breath, perhaps. But the piece is not over. The thematic material is still unresolved. Audiences do not begin premature applause in Bruckner's silences. They hold their breath, particularly during great performances in resonant halls. Then, after a few bars, the music begins again, quietly, mulling over the themes again to see what music can be extracted from them: a few strings, half the winds, an English horn. Bruckner orchestrates like an organist, pulling out stops, adding diapasons, opening the swell box, balancing masses of sound against each other. Thus begins another crescendo—another several minutes in which the music swells to even greater intensity and size. Then again, silence. Without those silences, that musical breathing, these remarkable pieces would not possess their power. Some find Bruckner a bit much, but I like my universe to have a little heft to it. I do not fear the sublime any more than silence. Bruckner, like Haydn, did not write music for waiting rooms, or for commercial messages. A single movement of Bruckner's Eighth Symphony would blow out the digital computer of Willmar—or Washington—or whoever else impugns your silence.

David Arnason once told me a story about silence. A film crew traveled across Iceland on a road named Sprengisandur, making a documentary for Canadian television. Originally a horse path traversing the country from southwest to east, it is now a jeep track through the high lava desert. The middle of Iceland is not a particularly hospitable place, though it is grandly beautiful in its starkness. Snow falls in every month of the year, and until midsummer the track is impassable. When American astronauts trained for their moon landing, they came to central Iceland—a landscape not unlike the one that awaited them.

Television crews always include a collection of "ambience," atmospheric sound intended to give the audience a sense of being actually present in nature. Ambience gathering is, of course, an act—or, if you wish, an art—of deception. Nature never sounds exactly like what your machine collects, but then what art—or political campaign or religious revival—doesn't depend on deception for its success? A television crew filming me once collected prairie noises on a summer afternoon: frog croaks, crickets, fly buzz, mosquito whine, wind in tall grass, the clacking of cottonwood leaves, a mourning dove moaning, a distant tractor. When I saw the program, I thought this was lovely, but I didn't remember any of those noises existing simultaneously. It was imagined, not actual, nature.

The ambience microphone is a sensitive and sophisticated piece of machinery. It can probably hear your breathing or the rustling of dollars in your billfold. At one point the TV crew stopped to photograph a particularly bleak and wild outcropping of bare lava, gravel, and boulders surrounded by lowering mountains and, probably, a glacier tongue or two. The ambience man grabbed his machine, put on his earphones, and, holding his microphone in front of him like a divining rod, walked off over the rough lava to collect ambience. He found, instead, intense silence. It was a rare windless day, no humans for fifty miles in any direction, no wandering animals or birds, no leaves, no running water, no grass. He looked at his machine in wonder—and frustration. Must be broken. The needle doesn't move. Not picking up a thing. Impossible. This isn't a vacuum chamber. Dammit, I'll have to walk back to the jeep and check the batteries. In frustration he slapped his thigh. The needle shot up as if a firecracker had exploded. It was nature that fooled him, not his machine. He had never been in the presence of such silence: complete confidentiality, as the nurse might have said. Say whatever you please, there's no one to hear it.

This silence in nature is, as Goethe suspected, a nourishing silence that fills human beings with joy, wisdom, calm, and the intuition of the inner life. This silence does not make us nervous. It does not need to be filled with chatter, jokes, news, or Muzak. We have all felt it at one time or another— maybe at the Grand Canyon, when we peer over the lip of the rim, or looking out over still water, or sometimes, for just a few seconds, after lovemaking, when two people lie back down together and then separate again without talk or even audible breathing. This is the silence Louis Simpson has in mind:

The Silent Piano

We have lived like civilized people.
O ruins, traditions!

And we have seen the barbarians,
breakers of sculpture and glass.

And now we talk of "the inner life,"
and I ask myself, where is it?

Not here, in these streets and houses,
so I think it must be found

in indolence, pure indolence,
an ocean of darkness,
in silence, an arm of the moon,
a hand that enters slowly.
...

I am reminded of a story
Camus tells, of a man in prison camp.

He had carved a piano keyboard
with a nail on a piece of wood.

And sat there playing the piano.
This music was made entirely of silence.

In the "streets and houses" the TV, or at least the radio, is on
with its empty noise. Maybe the cell phone rings to save us from
some interior plunge. Or a new soft-rock CD soothes us at the
flick of a knob. Maybe the man in the prison camp played Bach
on his silent piano, while the lines of music traveled from his
brain down through the spine and into the extraordinary, complex ganglia of nerves into the hands. And there he played the
Fugue in B Minor from Book I of the *Well-Tempered Clavier*.
Completely hidden from the ambience-collecting ears of the
camp guards.

I say nothing peculiar, outrageous, or unexpected. Indeed,
this is commonplace, something you already know. Every medi-
tative tradition confirms it—Buddhist, Judeo-Christian, Sufi,
and pagan. Let all mortal flesh keep silence. Then why, O why,
do you not go to your television set and your radio this very
minute, unplug them, open the window, and drop them out
from the greatest height in your house? While you are at it,
add the cell phone and the computer to the pile. They will
make a single, satisfying crash and you will be free.

But that's just foolishness, you say, no sense being so extreme. Besides, there are a lot of good programs on public television, BBC series are always excellent, we just watch sports events, we're careful with the children—only a few hours a day, it's good background while I'm working, it's really good for the old people in nursing homes. . . . O lord, the image of semidrugged bodies tied into wheelchairs with *As the World Turns*, *Oprah*, and Fox News nattering away. Give us the lead gift first!

I watched the Fox channel for a whole morning perhaps a month before the American invasion of Iraq. Because I see television so seldom, its effect on me is magnified. I cannot not pay attention to whatever blather passes over the screen. Heavy rain fell that morning, and so, as we say, there was nothing else to do. I tubed it—sitting in a comfortable leather chair, drinking Starbucks house blend, munching out of a bowl of pistachio nuts, half listening to the *obligato* of rain pounding on the roof. The motto for the day's news flashed on the screen every few minutes: TARGET: IRAQ! with quick shots of rolling tanks, bombs falling, flaming oil wells, and a little martial music.

That morning, with the actual invasion still more than a month away, the major story of the day was the administration's certainty that Saddam was hardly a baby's breath from building a nuclear bomb, and his hidden missiles were loaded with anthrax and smallpox, ready to go. The continual flashing of TARGET: IRAQ! at the bottom of the screen seemed to indicate that the invasion was a foregone conclusion, soon to be fact—and a great, quick triumph, whatever the objections of the rest of the planet. The terror alert had been raised to code orange—or was it red, or purple? I cannot remember the color sequence. Can you? Can anyone? And as a result, cars would be inspected on their approach to airports, shoes would be

X-rayed, fingernail clippers confiscated. "Alert authorities if you observe any unusual behavior." What would that be? Reading a book in public? Bellowing a Verdi aria to drown out your neighbor's cell phone?

Is the real work of television not to inform, calm, enlighten, or delight us, but, like the clinic's waiting-room Muzak, to keep us from actually thinking or communicating (that's "talk" in English) with each other in some simple, direct, and human way about the fruits of our experience and our reflections? Why, on that rainy morning, did the Fox channel (all channels) not mention the name of bin Laden—or of Ken Lay, one of the many scoundrels who sank Enron, stealing his own employees and stockholders clean? Or the ten other huge corporate scandals and bankruptcies that led—not entirely coincidentally—directly back to members of the administration, and that affected the economic health of all ordinary Americans? Our 401(k)s, our retirement billions, all seemed to be evaporating like rain in the desert. Wars cost money and ultimately bankrupt an empire. For empire we are. Not a simple little democratic experiment minding its own business, but the richest and most heavily armed empire in human history.

If a couple hours of this mental conditioning doesn't turn you into a complete neurotic, the "relief story" from Iraq on that rainy morning might finish the job. A dentist's wife somewhere in the vast middle of America stood trial for murdering her philandering husband with a Mercedes-Benz. When he stepped out into a hotel parking lot, hand in hand with his trophy-blond honey, the Mercedes suddenly slipped into gear and fast-forwarded over the dentist's skull. An accident caused by nervous grief, said the distraught but now remarkably composed wife. Murder one, said the district attorney. The jury had been out for a few hours. The network covered the courtroom closely, panning continually to the face of the aggrieved widow, then running an animated image of the Mercedes lurching across the parking lot toward the dentist. Lawyers and legal experts opined: "the longer they're out, the better her chance"; "could be a hung jury"; "should have gone for manslaughter or murder two." How could we ever arrive at any judgments in America without help from our talking heads, our experts, our professional opinionators?

The dentist's wife is guilty on all counts. The spokesman for the defense team comes on: "We're appealing! A miscarriage of justice!" A quick break for four or five commercials: allergy relief, laxatives, diet pills, exercise machines, depression lifters. Then back to TARGET: IRAQ! and code pink.

Let me propose two questions for your contemplation: First, in any room with a television set, who is watching whom? Do we watch Oprah, or does she watch us? Who is listening to whom in the clinic waiting room with its noisy confidentiality? Do the Dixie Chicks overhear our inmost secrets? These questions are not so silly as they first seem.

In a brilliant essay from 1984, "Big Brother Is You, Watching," Mark Crispin Miller argues persuasively that,

> ... we have become our own overseers. While Winston Smith is forced to watch himself in literal self-defense, trying to keep his individuality a hard-won secret, we have been forced to watch ourselves lest we develop selves too hard and secretive for the open market. In America, there is no need for an objective apparatus of surveillance (which is not to say that none exists), because, guided by TV, we watch ourselves as if already televised, checking ourselves both inwardly and outwardly for any sign of untidiness or gloom, moment by moment as guarded and self-conscious as Winston Smith under the scrutiny of the Thought Police. ...

But why? Miller continues:

> Television is not the cause of our habitual self-scrutiny,
> however, but has only set the standard for it, a relation-
> ship with a complicated history. It is through our ef-
> forts to maintain ourselves as the objects of our anxious
> self-spectatorship that we consummate the process of
> American Enlightenment, whose project throughout
> this century has been the complete and permanent re-
> duction of our populace into the collective instrument
> of absolute production. This project has arisen not
> through corporate conspiracy but as the logical fulfill-
> ment, openly and even optimistically pursued, of the
> imperative of unlimited economic growth.

It is perhaps hardly surprising in this light that the Patriot
Act, the most frightening—and least American—legislation
in American history (I do not exempt the Alien and Sedition
Acts or even the Jim Crow laws), seemed to be passively accepted by a numbed citizenry. Miller agrees that we have already been softened up nicely for harvesting by the complete
security state. As he explains:

> ... Americans have been closely watched for decades:
> in the factory, then in the office, by efficiency experts
> and industrial psychologists; in the supermarkets, then
> throughout the shopping malls, by motivational re-
> searchers no less cunningly than by the store detectives;
> in the schools, and then at home, and then in bed, by an
> immense, diverse, yet ultimately unified bureaucracy of
> social workers, education specialists, and "mental health
> professionals" of every kind. . . . Americans—restless, dis-
> connected, and insatiable—are mere consumers, having
> by now internalized the diffuse apparatus of surveillance

built all around them, while still depending heavily on its external forms—TV, psychologistic "counseling," "self-help" manuals, the "human potential" regimens, and other self-perpetuating therapies administered to keep us on the job.

Miller's essay is partly a survey of the many misreadings of *1984*. In closing he writes:

> In too many ways, the ex-hero of this brilliant, dismal book anticipates those TV viewers who are incapable of reading it: "In these days he could never fix his mind on any one subject for more than a few moments at a time."

Ask any classroom teacher about the state of mental discipline in most American students at the moment. Assign a book, then give a simple quiz: What happened? When or where? Who were the main characters? What is the subject of this book? When the failed quizzes are returned, listen to the curious and puzzled response: But I read the book—the whole thing. The student does not lie. He turned the pages, and his interior dictionary registered the meaning of the words; if a murder was committed, he probably noticed it. But the interior connections, the tone of the language, the humor, the thread that binds a book to the reader's life—these and more register a silence as absolute as what the ambience man found on Sprengisandur. I'm afraid it's hard to sustain high hope for literature in the twenty-first century. We may be reduced to wringing the poetry out of technical manuals and federal security alerts.

I keep my personal silence in the sitting room of Brimnes. My yellow couch faces the big window looking out to sea and to a thirteen-mile-long, thirty-five-hundred-foot loaf of mountain.

Tindastóll says nothing. On calm days the fjord is equally quiet, but with a vigorous northwest or southwest wind loud breakers roll fiercely onto the gravel beach. About two hundred feet north of the house, the Hof River surges noisily into the sea at the end of its ten-mile course from the small glacier at the head of Unadalur Valley. Once a day in calm weather, the outrushing river and the incoming tide reach a kind of silent stasis, a spiritual and hydrological harmony where, for a while, nothing more need be said. A couple hundred eider ducks, who nest out of sight on a beach around the corner of the little basalt cliff, gather close to shore, purring and clucking as they teach their chicks to dive and catch fish in calm water. The eiders are quiet, peaceful birds, mumbling so softly that except in extremely calm weather I can't hear them even from fifty yards away. A pair of ravens visit a few times a week, and they are unashamedly noisy. I miss their harsh, guttural song when they stay away too long, but I don't want them here night and day. Schoenberg has his own beauty if you hear him now and then, but no one wants a solid week of this raven composer. The shrill terns—the kría—fish daily in the oncoming tide, and shout about their luck at the top of their lungs. On sunny afternoons a few whimbrels and plovers stroll, warbling and trilling, through the grass under the window. I've heard thunder only once in Iceland, and the noise shocked the natives. Some claimed never to have heard it at all, or were not sure what it was. Here, thunderstorms happen only in Beethoven symphonies or in books.

In this room, the only noise is the ticking of a small clock. I wanted an audible tick in this otherwise silent house, to be reminded of time passing. I mistrust digital clocks, which exist in an eternal numerical present. I want always to know what time it is and what time it will be, and I want a circle and hands to make a visible metaphor for time. I miss the old

Regulator clocks—with their heavy wood cases, glass doors, and winding keys—that hung in railroad depots, post offices, hardware stores, and the parlors of my great-aunts. When I bought this feeble excuse for a Regulator at the Sauðárkrókur Cooperative Store (the Icelandic version of Target), I insisted that the clerk play me the ticks on his whole selection of clocks so that I could at least choose a small voice to mark the passage of hours.

Brimnes is without television, computer, phone (cell or regular), VCR, or radio. A cheap CD player and fifty or sixty discs stand mostly unused—and always silent whenever human beings are present. If I am practicing music by a particular composer, I play the disc and follow the music in score. Late at night, when I am alone, I sometimes play one of fifteen or twenty recordings of Haydn quartets for an hour. I do not read—or even daydream. I often pour a whiskey or cognac, stare out the window at the late pink light on the cliffs and water, and listen to what Haydn has to say. He has never bored or disappointed me.

A small Yamaha upright stands in the corner of the next room. It is not a beautiful piano, the strings too short to resonate, the bass dull, the treble shrill. But it is tuned and music can be made with it. It is a satisfactory instrument when you are more interested in training your fingers for accuracy than in making lovely noises. Each summer I work at a large, difficult piece or two, competing with the ravens and the terns. Last summer I learned Prokofiev's Sonata no. 9 in C Major; this summer I am thumping away at Hindemith's First Sonata and Medtner's Tenth Sonata. Between these large pieces, I practice Bach fugues. No pianist should die without having had a try at all forty-eight of them.

Sometimes musicians visit Brimnes. My old friend Anna Sigga Helgadóttir is, if not Iceland's best mezzo-soprano, its most versatile and soulful. A recording of her singing arias from Bach's *Christmas Oratorio* once cured my cousin Daren Gíslason's sinus infection. I do not doubt this fact, though it is not necessarily supported by science. When Anna Sigga comes to Brimnes, we read—what great pleasure!—songs of Brahms, Schumann, Dvorák, Britten, and Icelandic composers. Her voice so fills the room with feeling and beauty that guests—and often the piano player—begin weeping in spontaneous joy.

A former student of my friend Wincie arrived in Hofsós with his wife and two small children on a camping trip. Wincie introduced us: "Stebbi is a professional cellist," she said.

"Good," said I. "Bring your cello to Brimnes and we'll read some sonatas—Brahms if you've got him along." But Stebbi had neglected to bring even his cello. Too bad.

"Wait." He remembered he had an old student twenty miles away in Sauðárkrókur. "I'll borrow his cello." That night he came to Brimnes with cello in hand, but no score until tomorrow.

"Then play some Bach you know," we all said.

Bach in Brimnes

Stebbi brings his cello into Brimnes.
He is a big thick fellow with ham fists
who looks like a seaman, some deck hand
more used to tubs of fish than cello bows.
No scores here, so he'll play what he knows.
Bach! Let's have a little Bach: a Saraband.
The cello seems too big for this small room
but when he starts the Saraband in G
the whole house grows too tiny for the tune,
as if the walls were pressing to expand
another fifty paces toward the sea

to make a breathing space for all this sound,
if any human space we build could house
whatever whirls around inside this suite.

But Hofsós does not exist in a pastoral idyll. The internal combustion engine is here, and every Hofsósingur seems to own at least one car, jeep, or truck. They are few enough, though, to escape the din of traffic jams, honking horns, freeway rumble. One local collector owns an almost-mint '59 charcoal Cadillac Fleetwood. What a glorious past those soaring tail fins conjure!

Hofsós is surrounded by working farms, dairy cows, horses, sheep, and always a home hay field—the *tún*—thus, in season, the distant putting of tractors, clanking of rakes, the slap of the hay-binding machine, and now and then the thundering hooves of a pasture full of horses galloping together in high spirits.

The now-underused harbor still provides berth for one good-sized and four or five small fishing trawlers, but they enter and leave so quietly that one only becomes aware of them by watching the puffs of diesel smoke. A waggish pilot who keeps his homemade hobby plane in the next fjord sometimes feints dive-bombing the houses of his friends in Hofsós. The plane sounds like an aerial machine gun. "Oh, it's just Arngrímur having a good time." No one seems hysterical about terrorist threats arriving from the sky in Skagafjörður. Osama bin Laden must have better things to do farther south of the Arctic Circle. The sky is mostly unmarked by jet trails. That's a good sign.

One twenty-first-century monster does flourish here—the weed whacker. Why the suburban fancy for butch-cut grass surfaced in—of all places!—Iceland is a mystery to me, but here it is, present in size and majesty. Icelandic grass is remarkable.

How Walt Whitman would have loved it! It flourishes only in its little season of light and warmth, from June to mid-August. It is the hay that has fed the sheep and kept the nation alive for a thousand years. Its refusal to grow in the cold summer of the 1870s led first to starvation and poverty, and ultimately to the huge emigration to Canada and the United States. What a strange idea—that the absence of grass drove my grandparents to Minneota—Bill Holm, a stepchild of the grass.

The wild grass in Minnesota is hard textured, spiky, full of brambles and burrs, often crawling with garter snakes, and covered with a cloud of mostly unpleasant biting insects. If you want an outdoor nap, bring a thick blanket and plenty of insect poison. But the grass in Iceland is soft as a mattress, full of a dozen wildflowers, occasionally patrolled—on sunny days—by a few nonstinging midges and sleepy flies. A grassy hillside on a sunny afternoon is the sweetest bed you have ever dozed in.

Enter the weed whacker. A lawn mower is noise enough, but the weed whacker—invented, I suppose, to trim steep hillsides and tight spots impervious to ordinary mower blades—raises the noise ante to the level of pure pain. In Hofsós, they have come to be the mower of choice for all grass. The township hires local teenagers for summer community work: painting, mowing, washing, planting. It is hard to imagine, when they come dressed to whack, that inside their costumes live handsome Icelandic teenagers. They look like malicious space aliens in some science-fiction horror movie—or like the book-burning team in Antonioni's *Fahrenheit 451*. Sheathed head to foot in heavy padded coveralls, big padded mittens, a face guard that's a cross between a welder's helmet and a goalie's mask, oversized padded ear guards—the greatest necessity of all in this modern knight's armor—and, finally, clumpy moon boots, probably steel toed. The outfit alone must cost a fortune, much less the very expensive whackers themselves, and either the gas or electricity necessary to feed them. All this to rid the world of a little shaggy grass and a bumper crop of dandelions, to make uniformity from chaos.

The whacker wields his weapon like an air hammer, or a Gatling gun aimed downward into the earth. When the motor catches, the noise begins. It clearly requires muscle to hold and maneuver the monster, and the whacker knight extends his arms in a wide upside-down *V* to grasp the weapon's handles. This is no job for a one-armed man or woman. If you sneeze or daydream or lose control, those whirling rotary blades could probably whack off your toes in half a second, maybe even inside your steel-toed boots. The whacker moves deliberately over the hillside. No need to hurry this serenade. The machine misses neither dandelion nor daisy nor poppy nor marigold nor grass blade. After what seems, to any neighbors in earshot, an eternity, you will have given your hillside a crew cut—it's ready for Marine boot camp now. But even decimated flowers and grass return to life, and you will have to repeat your whacking soon, over and over and over, until frost and snow retire your motorized snarler to its coffin before it rises again in the spring.

I, for one, would gladly drive a stake through the whacker's metal heart, and while I probably would not receive the Nobel Noise Control Prize from my neighbors, I would—I say in all humility—certainly deserve it. The violent intensity of this noise cannot be described without resorting to metaphor. It is almost beyond language. It is a gigantic, powerful dentist's drill performing a deep and difficult root canal at the back of your mouth—sans novocaine—but with the drill noise amplified, as if through the giant speakers of a punk heavy-metal band, until your eardrums seem likely to explode from pain. It carries a mile, though from that distance it is reduced to the dull whining of a cloud of elephantine mosquitoes. Any place within a quarter-mile radius is unbearable—though you, of course, have to bear it. Whackers "share" their song with or without your consent. Only rain and cold spare you; on any sunny day in season, they emerge, generally just as midafternoon has made the idea of a nap irresistible. Resist it.

My antiwhacker harangues irritate my old friend and fellow transplanted Hofsósingur Wincie. Nothing but Luddite raving, she says, and I'm tired of it. Grow up and live in your own century. What do you want them to use? A scythe? Indeed! That's it, exactly, and a grand old Anglo-Saxon word it is, with its archaic and irrational spelling. Its image is darkened a little by its symbolic representation as the tool of the Angel of Death, the Grim Reaper, with which he intends to gather you yourself—when the time is ripe—into his own hay crop of souls. Better he should gather you with the swoosh of the almost-silent scythe than with the violent-voiced whacker. Imagine the whacker singing the gentle "In Paradisum" from Fauré's Requiem or the last pages of *Faust* set by Gustav Mahler in Symphony no. 8. When I am scythed, let Anna Sigga sing and Stebbi play Bach, and let the whacker—and the clinic Muzak and the Fox channel—keep silence. Let them maintain confidentiality in themselves—forever.

Samuel Johnson said, "It is always a writer's duty to make the world better, and justice is a virtue independent of time and place." After Johnson penned that trumpet of a sentence, the Industrial Revolution arrived, followed soon after by the modern media and modern armaments (WMDs), and the whole panoply of gadgets birthed by technology. We now mostly sit in closed rooms in front of flashing screens, doing the duty of commercial and bureaucratic interests, watching pictures of a nature that we have almost managed, in our ignorance and greed, to destroy completely. We have done this by letting whatever is wise inside us be deadened and manipulated by the loud Muzak of machines programmed by authority. If we sat in silence—or simple human talk—in the clinic waiting room, and if we thought long and hard in that silence on whether our country should thump its way through the world with its army, then maybe a real sense of justice "independent of time and place" could be born inside us.

A GIFT OF HORSES

A student foolhardy enough to attempt the study of Icelandic, a forbiddingly inflected language with enough grammar to sink a champion linguist, begins with this direction: decline the strong noun *horse*, or *að beygja nafnorðið hestur* (masculine).

nom.	hér er hestur (here is (a) horse)
acc.	um hest (about a horse)
dat.	frá hesti (from a horse)
gen.	til hests (to a horse, on horseback)
nom.	hér eru hestar (here are horses)
acc.	um hesta (about some horses)
dat.	frá hestum (from some horses)
gen.	til hesta (to some horses)

Horse is the first word, and in many ways also a good first fact, if you are to understand a little the peculiarity of Iceland.

In 1979 I taught American literature at the University of Iceland in Reykjavík. That October, my old Minneota friend John Allen arrived to have a look at Iceland. John is both an athlete and a traveler. His love of nature and wilderness inspired him (over the course of several years) to walk both the Pacific Crest and the Continental Divide trails from Canada to Mexico, then the Great River Road, following the Mississippi from Lake Itasca to the Gulf of Mexico. It didn't take him long to notice the immense and then almost-empty beauty of Iceland, and to hatch a plan to walk and hitchhike around the entire country. At that time Highway 1, or the Ring Road was often the only road through vast stretches of the country. And for much of its length (one thousand miles) it was hardly a road at all, only a few tarred miles, then rough one-and-a-half-lane gravel, then long stretches of ruts, mud, and stones that stopped many a journey short. The southeast section had only recently been bridged, thus making John's scheme of a ring possible. My students assured him that he had lost his mind, that October was a dangerous month with chancy weather, that the road was lonely and very lightly traveled, and that once he left Reykjavík he would hear little English. But he behaved like an Icelander and decided to do it anyway.

He already knew two useful words of Icelandic. Like most foreigners, he'd sampled the Icelander's favorite national dish, the lamb hot dog, but again like most of us, he found remoulade (a sweet, sticky pink mayonnaise) unsatisfactory. How to get a hot dog without it? My students taught him *ekki remoulade*—no remoulade! Without having memorized the declension myself, I assured John that *hestur* might be the most useful word in Icelandic. And so, armed with three words and a fearless spirit, he set off in mid-October.

I met him in Egilsstaðir (halfway around the country), having flown east to see friends. Not surprisingly, John had already had several fine adventures. He'd met a beautiful woman on the south coast who gave him a ride. "She looked like Liv Ullman," he said. He'd been invited to stay at a farm in one of the eastern fjords. He'd dined on sheep's head and toured a shark-drying house. He reported that the shark tasted terrible, but that it was possible with schnapps.

I found him a ride over the worst part of the lava desert to Akureyri with an old trucker who fed him salted boiled sheep's knuckles and regaled him with stories—in Icelandic. He understood not a word. At Hrútafjörður, he picked up a ride with a salesman—all the way to Reykjavík. Here's the whole conversation: "Reykjavík?" "Reykjavík, já." "Takk." Fortunately, John did get to use his Icelandic. When they passed one of the multitude of horse farms along the road, he perked up, pointed, and said, "hestur." "Já, já . . . hestur," said the salesman. When they reached Reykjavík after four or five hours, they shook hands, having established a friendship of a kind, and John called me to pick him up. My students were impressed with his courageous achievement—circling the whole country in October. "I owe it to the hestur," he said modestly.

I can't see horses out the windows of Brimnes, but they are more numerous than humans in Skagafjörður. Occasionally local horsemen ride down the steep lane behind the house. I turn my back to the fjord and the mountains, and look out the kitchen window to see them coming downhill. Sometimes they show off by riding up and down five times to demonstrate for delighted onlookers the five gaits of the Icelandic horse: first the walk (*fet*), then pace (*skeið*), trot (*brökk*), gallop (*stökk*), and finally the famous *tölt*, a running walk so smooth and precise that the rider sits erect and perfectly still in the saddle with no bouncing or tossing. Sigurður A. Magnússon, one of Iceland's distinguished men of letters and an enthusiastic rider and chronicler of the Icelandic horse, describes it this way: "The tölt is a gait with quartered beat with equal intervals and the footfalls are: back left, front left, back right, front right. . . . It is a gait that with unaltered footfall can escalate its swiftness from a mere step to great speed. One hears the tölt distinctly as a constant four-beat staccato; one sees it also; the horse is proudly erect and carries its tail in a typically undulating movement." I like Sigurður's musical metaphor. It sounds to me like riding on the back of the bass line in a Bach concerto. At home, play the B Minor Prelude from

Well-Tempered Clavier I with a staccato bass. You will hear the tölt. Music made visible, topped by a fine riding habit, white breeches, shiny black boots, a red jacket, and a pert black riding helmet. No other European horse has such a gait; you have to go as far as Mongolia to find it again, in the horses of another almost-desert.

Around the age of fifty, my old friend Jón fell into a happy marriage to Elín, a lovely woman in her forties. She owns a horse farm in south Skagafjörður, famous for its hot water that bubbles to the surface everywhere, giving rise to clouds of misty steam, and for its history as a large, prosperous Benedictine convent in the Middle Ages. The convent owned fifty farms and a large library until it was sacked by the king of Denmark in 1552. He claimed the property and evicted the nuns. Hundreds of years of nun bones must sleep under all that mysterious hot water. For a wedding present, Elín gave Jón a spirited-looking black stallion.

Skagfirðingur—the locals in this fjord—like to brag about three of their skills: they are singers, drinkers, and horsemen. Indeed, it hardly requires even a few drinks before they are singing, usually in four parts. They sing of the blue skies of Skagafjörður; of the local mountains, Tindastóll or Mælifell; of the plover's song, riding songs, drinking songs, love songs. And they sing very well. The local men's choir, Heimir, will inform you that they are the finest in Iceland. Maybe true, maybe not, but they surely sing with vigor, no shyness or diffidence or coaxing necessary. Four brothers from a local farm, Álftagerði—three Italian tenors and almost-a-baritone—are Iceland's best-loved men's quartet, singing sentimental, national, and dance songs. Even the small country churches have lovely voices in their choirs. Not surprisingly, there's a fine music education program active all over the district.

And they are very accomplished horsemen—and horse-women. Skagafjörður has some of the richest pastureland and hay fields in Iceland, and the stud farms, riding stables, and huge herds everywhere testify to it. It's lovely to drive by a wide pasture with a hundred or so horses. I sometimes stop to try to count the colors: black, gray, white, roan, chest-nut, red, brown, cream, various shades and piebald combinations, with yet more colors on manes and tails. If you stop the car and walk to the fence line, you will soon be greeted by a lineup of curious horses looking you in the eye. It brings Walt Whitman's line to mind: "The look of the bay mare shames the silliness out of me."

You can even major in horse in Skagafjörður. Hólar, the old bishopric in Hjaltadalur, offers a three-year degree in Equine Studies at the School of the Icelandic Horse. After graduation, you can start your own school—training and taming these half-wild creatures. The river from Hólar runs ten miles through a lovely canyon to Kolkuós. Probably the oldest Viking anchorage in Iceland, this protected hook in the river's mouth is an ancient farm site, and now the scene of a big archeological dig to unearth the remains of a thousand years of settlement and trade. Evidence suggests that the first Norwegian horses landed here off the longboats. The horses still look happy to me, galloping in their Kolkuós pasture, as if they had gotten used to this place after a millenium.

A caravan of emigrants left Mjóidalur (Narrow Valley) in Þingeyjarsýsla, two counties east of Brimnes, in July, 1873, intending to join a larger group from Bárðardalur. Twenty were bound for North America, twenty for Brazil. Their first destination was Akureyri, the northern port town, to meet the *Queen,* a Scottish steamer that would leave in late July. The

Queen's cargo consisted mostly of horses and emigrants. Among the travelers was Stefán Guðmundsson, twenty years old, born in Skagafjörður a half-hour's drive from Brimnes, and later to become Stephan G. Stephansson, the greatest of the Icelandic emigrant poets.

Some sold their farms to raise the eighty-four *ríkisdalur* fare to the New World, but Stephan's parents, Guðmundur and Guðbjörg, owned no land, only a little livestock. They sold their sheep and horses to Gránafélag, a trading company that had made a contract with Slimon Brothers, a company from Leith, to supply great numbers of Icelandic horses for the British mining industry. The Slimon brothers also owned the *Queen*. Icelandic horses were much valued in British pit mines. They were small, strong, and intelligent. They were winched underground by chain (no mine elevators yet) at night, to prepare them for their future: blindfolded in the subterranean blackness, pulling ore carts, until they actually went blind, after which, presumably, the blindfolds could be removed. Icelandic horses continued to labor in the mines until the late 1930s, when they were replaced by machinery.

The emigrant caravan crossed Fnjóskadalur just east of Akureyri on July 17 in a fierce snowstorm. Their emigrant chests—likely containing a few woolen garments, some rough wooden tools, perhaps some wood spoons and bowls, maybe an eiderdown quilt, and all the books they owned or could carry—were strapped to the backs of the horses they were selling to buy their passage. Their last pack trip in the Old World. The homemade wood boxes, square with a strap hole, were called *koffort* (trunk) or *kista* in Icelandic, the same word for "coffin." I still own the kista my grandfather carried aboard ship from Vopnafjörður in 1879. Like Stephansson, he was twenty years old. His family's horses were probably sold, like Stephansson's, to the Slimon brothers for passage money, and thence into some Welsh coal pit. Someone in the intervening years has painted the kista blue. I use it as a nightstand by my bed to hold piles of books to browse before sleep. The kista is empty now, and it no longer smells even faintly of horse sweat.

On August 2, 1873, the *Queen* sailed from Akureyri with 153 Icelanders in steerage (first class was occupied mostly by English travelers—tourists returning from quaint and exotic Iceland), and 220 horses, including the farm horses sold by our little band of emigrants. The ship's hold, just below steerage, was filled with horses packed tightly together, and those that couldn't fit below were tethered on the open deck, chained to the ship so they didn't go berserk and leap or fall into the sea. A canvas funnel meant to fumigate the horse smell failed to work, so Stephansson said (ironically), "You could easily get a pleasant smell from the nether regions." Guðmundur, Stephan's father, stood out on deck to watch the farms he knew so well disappear one by one as the *Queen* steamed north in Eyjafjörður, toward the open sea. But a dense fog descended, as it often still does. When the ship reached open water, still shrouded in fog after three days, a southwest gale came up to rile the sea. Many passengers stood on deck, listening to the heaving of seasick Icelanders below and the frenzied whinnies and hoof stomping of the packed in, seasick horses. These horses belonged to them—they were almost pets, childhood companions whose backs they'd straddled and whose noses they'd stroked. The *Queen* was to land fifteen horses at Lerwick in the Shetlands, but by the time the ship arrived a few of them were already dead. Guðmundur said he "often wished that all of them would die. . . . They were beautiful creatures. The horses were fed a little hay every twenty-four hours (never enough) but no water. They strained their necks whenever water was carried along the deck, but neither I nor any others could help them. The crew did not allow us to interfere; they simply left the horses to struggle until they collapsed and died."

On August 9, they arrived at Aberdeen, where all the remaining horses were unloaded and the Icelanders herded together aboard their first train to Glasgow, then Liverpool, for the final leg of the voyage to Quebec. Blessedly, there were no horses aboard the transoceanic steamship. Gránufélagið and the shipping company raised the fares for the Icelanders for this first sea trip at the last minute, so they found themselves penniless as they set out to begin their adventure in the New World.

I try to imagine what must have been going through the minds of those wretchedly poor but literate emigrants, leaving their culture, language, family, and landscape to start over in the great unknown. What kind of thoughts passed through their minds in the sea fog? Did their consciences sting from having traveled over the North Atlantic directly above their suffering horses? Were America and Canada a spiritual mine shaft they were descending, to be blindfolded forever until daylight made no difference? My grandparents rode ships like the *Queen,* in their case the *Camoens,* listening to the uneasy writhing and smelling the shit of their own horses. What did they think?

The Icelandic horses, like the Icelanders themselves, had just survived their second emigrant trip in a thousand years. Indeed, if horses possessed some ancestral or archetypal memory, these might have remembered their first oceanic emigration, from Norway to Iceland, some eight hundred years before. Each time a little farther west, to something new that might look better than what they had left. Or not. Americans are foolish to imagine that immigrants always come gladly, or that they are eager to "melt." People do not immigrate for "freedom," an SUV, welfare payments, or our gods (however you understand them), or even for the chance to speak English, drink Coke, wear Levis, and eat McDonald's hamburgers. People more often emigrate because they are desperate, and there is nothing left for them in the Old World. And some, like the dead Icelandic horses heaved into the sea, will not survive the experience.

One pink June night recently, I came within a minute or two of seeing a foal arrive in the world. My friend Gunna (Guðrún Þórvaldsdóttir) from Vatn is a horse farmer, too, if on a smaller scale. She has a few horses and she loves them dearly. A carload of us were driving past Vatn with Gunna's husband, Valgeir, when he suddenly hit his brakes. I think we should meet this new horse, he said. We clambered over the fence to Gunna, who stood next to a spindly, tan colt, still damp from the amniotic sac that lay in a glop next to him. He tried to stand up, succeeded briefly, then toppled over again and lay there looking around at us, his first humans, along with the mountains, lake, and sea, his eyes probably still a bit cloudy from his trip down the birth canal. The mare stood a yard or two away, peacefully munching mouthful after mouthful of spring grass. We stood admiring the scene for a few minutes. A wet string of umbilical cord hung from the back end of the calmly munching mare. We walked back toward the fence. Gunna stopped to inspect with her hands the belly of another mare. Not quite ready to foal. "This is my horse," said Gunna, "a gift from my father." I know nothing about horses or how to judge them one from another, but this horse was a beauty, piebald roan and white with an enormous mane—pure white, snow white, ice white, ghost white, whiter than any white—and looking out from under that mane two of the deepest eyes I've ever seen— deep brown, almost black. We all stood there silently, admiring this handsome mare. I think I fell in love—with a horse! Is it possible? James Wright seems to have done it in literature,

and maybe in life: "If I stepped out of my body I would break /
Into blossom." I asked Gunna the mare's name. "Lukka," she
said. Luck. It's a good name, for horse or human being.

The old Norse gods made the same mistake as the ancient
Chinese (and as the Israelis and we Americans today). They
wanted a wall around their territory to defend it from the
Giants. Substitute your own enemy. They made a small error in
hiring a builder, however, since (unknown to them) the builder
was kin to the Giant clan. Loki, the shape-shifter and mischief
maker of the gods, arranged the contract. The wall-smith had
three years to complete the project and could use no help but
his cart horse Svaðilfari, or he would lose everything. For his
fee, should he complete it, he would get the sun, the moon,
and the goddess Freyja. The gods were bound by oaths on the
contract.

The builder and his cart horse worked with such persis-
tence that they seemed likely to finish the wall within the time
alotted. The gods were furious with Loki, so he devised a trick:
he turned himself into a mare and, on the last night, popped
out to whinny seductively at the cart horse—who promptly
broke his tether, dropped his load of stones, and disappeared
into the woods with the perky new mare. The builder lost. The
sun and the moon and Freyja were saved. Thor came with his
hammer and smashed the giant's skull to splinters. But Loki,
the trickster, got his own comeuppance: he was pregnant by
the giant's stallion. He gave birth to a monster, an eight-legged
foal who grew up to be the famous Sleipnir, Odin's favorite
horse.

Sleipnir is possessed of talents beyond an ordinary Icelandic
horse. Odin can summon Sleipnir merely by thinking of him.
When he does, the mind-reading horse tölts into Valhalla,
ready to ride. One day Odin met the giant Rungnir on his own

steed, Golden Mane. "What warrior are you," asked Rungnir, "with golden helmet, riding on an eight-legged steed, passing at will through air and water?" Odin identified himself and challenged the giant to a horse race. He wagered his head. The giant accepted and they raced, Sleipnir speeding through clouds, spurning the mountaintops with his hooves. Odin and Sleipnir won the race, of course, after which he invited the giant in for a drink. Thor wound up having to kill this one with his hammer, too—little brother mopping up for his arrogant and foolish big brother.

You will surely recognize the pair of them, Odin and Sleipnir, if they canter into your yard. Odin is a tall man with one eye and one empty socket, clad in a black cloak, his shoulders holding two large ravens (Thought and Memory). The horse has eight legs and appears riding out of a cloud. You don't see that every day. He's actually Odin's nephew— ættfræði again!

The sagas are full of horse stories, too, *Hrafnkel Priest of Frey* the most famous of them. Hrafnkel was a rich, arrogant farmer (a chieftain) whose favorite possession was "a pale-dun stallion with a black mane and a black stripe down back. He called the horse Freyfaxi and gave his patron Frey [the god] a half-share in it." He made an oath to himself (and presumably to Freyr) to kill anyone who tried to ride Freyfaxi. One of his hired shepherds, caught in a pinch, rode him back to the farm. Hrafnkel found the horse breathless, muddy, and sweating. "Who rode him?" he asked. Einar owned up to it. "Why did you ride this one horse which was forbidden you, when there were plenty of other horses you were free to ride? I'd have forgiven this single offence if I'd not sworn so great an oath." At which point he buried his axe in Einar's head.

The forbidden fruit, the devil's apple. It's an old story. Hrafnkel, like Adam and Eve, suffered severe consequences for his foolish oath. He lost all his wealth in a lawsuit and suffered personal humiliation, though he wasn't killed. That was a mistake, because Hrafnkel was a man of high quality—breeding tells, in men as in stallions. He regained all his wealth and power, finally exacting revenge on his tormentors for humiliating him, and returned to his chieftaincy, and his old farm in the district. Freyfaxi, however, suffered from Hrafnkel's obstinacy. His enemies thought that no more men should suffer death for this horse, so they led him to a high bluff, fastened a stone to his neck, and, with poles, pushed the horse over the cliff. That bluff, the saga tells us, has been called Freyfaxihamar ever since. Sleipnir could fly through the clouds; Freyfaxi, with only four legs, couldn't.

The son of an old friend in Reykjavík has fallen in love with horses. He owns a small herd of them, stabling and pasturing them on the outskirts of the city. I once asked him what use a fellow who sold furniture had for all those horses. We ride them, he said, and indeed, on fine summer days, hundreds of them tölt around the Reykjavík countryside carrying children of all ages. And we sell them, he said. Indeed, there is a lively market for Icelandic horses all over the world. They are admired for their beauty, intelligence, and hardiness. Several of my neighbors in Minnesota buy and breed these horses. They even come to Iceland for roundups and to visit the farms that produce their stock. The horse trade nets the national economy a nice gathering of dollars and euros each year. And finally, we eat them, he said. They are delicious, particularly foal steaks—as tender, sweet, and flavorful as any prime beef. Country people are particularly fond of salted horse, claiming that it keeps their blood healthy through the long dark winters. The tastiest salamis are made from *folaldakjöt*—foal meat.

Shocked, are you? The rest of the planet—excepting Britain and America—has always enjoyed horse meat. Horse sushi is prized in Japan, and Paris boasts of horse butchers. We Americans could use a bit less squeamishness. The early Christian church tried to forbid the eating of horse meat in Iceland, even having the parliament declare it a punishable crime. The prohibition worked as well as prohibitions usually do—whether it be alcohol, tobacco, dangerous literature, obscene music, ad infinitum. The Icelanders ignored the law and continued to enjoy their horse dinners, all the while loving their horses.

Well into the twentieth century, the horse was still the main vehicle for getting from one place to another in Iceland, and for transporting goods to places that couldn't be reached by sea. My neighbor Hallgrímur remembers going to a confirmation at a country church a few hours north of Reykjavík in the fifties, with the whole large family arriving on horseback. No cars and no real roads to drive them on.

The Icelandic horse is a wild animal for at least its first three or four years, until it is trained for riding and working. It runs free in its pastures or high in the mountains in summer, and then is wrangled downhill in September. It's a pretty good life for a horse. Icelandic hay—only ordinary grass, really—is tasty and nutritious, the water is clear, cold, and pure in every river, and salt can be licked off driftwood fence posts. Icelanders have written thousands of romantic poems and sung songs about horses. What's your call, friend horse? Your underbelly girdled by a sling, feet (only four, unless you are Sleipnir) dangling in midair, winched over and dropped into the hold of a Slimon steamer? Or the dinner table? It's probably not a good choice, but then most choices in this imperfect world aren't. In the first case, you provide money to the desperately poor and labor for the mine owner, and in the second you provide pleasure and nourishment. There will be skáls to you with wine—or schnapps—and praise for your delicious flavor. Take and eat. No choice here.

CHRISTIANITY UNDER
THE GLACIER

Sunday morning in early July, a day of some sun but even more blustering rain, shot at the windows by fierce wind as if out of the barrel of some cosmic water cannon. All over Iceland, the churches are mostly empty. A baptism here and there, or perhaps a confirmation, will bring out a family or two or three. Afterward a fine party: cream cakes, gravlax, smoked mutton on flatbread, *brauðterta* (a huge, layered sandwich with shrimp, eggs, and mayonnaise), coffee, and sometimes a little schnapps. Usually the priest comes, whoever she might be (lots of clergywomen these days—and gay ones, too). Grace will not be said. Praying over food is not customary in Icelandic homes. Prayers are for children to say before bed, or to be read accurately in a long, dry voice, out of a heavy book, at a funeral. Usually the choir loft is well populated and the singing of high quality: Bach, Bruckner, Mendelssohn, Þorkell Sigurbjörnsson (or another of the multitude of Icelandic choral composers) ringing out over the mostly deserted pews. Sometimes, after the liturgical responses and anthem and before the sermon, the choir loft thins out. Singing in chorus is an Icelandic national habit—and passion—with a long and honorable lineage, but preaching homilies is often a dull science. There are no altar calls, no shaking and rattling, no waving of arms, no shouted hallelujahs, and no noisy evangelical fervor at all in the Icelandic church. Choir singing is civil service in Iceland's state Lutheran church, and thus serving one's fellow Icelanders in the alto section entails some compensation. One choir I know pools these funds, and then uses them for an annual trip: sometimes Poland, Germany, or Spain, or even around Iceland itself, where they sing well-received concerts including much new Icelandic music. Not often is it possible to serve god and the state simultaneously—with a clear conscience and a sense of honor—but the Icelanders seem to manage quite well.

After the benediction, the choir, and whatever congregation has assembled, stays put to hear the organ postlude, maybe a Bach Prelude and Fugue. I last heard the big C Major in the cozy Reykjavík cathedral. Not a soul stirred until the four voices of the fugue strettoed their way triumphantly to the final cadence—followed by justly deserved applause. Who would have thought spiritual experience possible in a stuffy state church? The organists and choirmasters are civil servants, too, along with the priests, of course. Even the organs themselves are the property of Iceland. I've heard magnificent organs at many Reykjavík and suburban churches, and I'm told that every half-sizeable town in the country boasts good ones, too. The tiny country churches are serviced by small harmoniums, pump organs—like those in the American churches of my boyhood. No electricity required, only strong, energetic knees and a mouse-hole-free bellows. The harmonium has a sweet and nostalgic sound—its own brand of national service to history—but not much use in bringing off the grand finale of the C Major Fugue. It's better for slow funeral hymns like "Allt eins og blómstrið eina"— "just as the flower withers, so does the body pass away." It's an Icelandic favorite.

The wedding hymns here are slow and sad. Before I understood much of what went on in Icelandic, I heard my good friend the mezzo-soprano Anna Sigga Helgadóttir rehearsing a lugubrious-sounding minor-key adagio solo for her church.

Who died, I inquired? No one died, she huffed; this is a wedding song. There are not many tambourines in the Icelandic church, not much finger snapping, few drum sets, nary a rock-guitar mass over the whole country—just a few wheezy *tremolo vox humana* stops on the old harmoniums.

Listening one rainy Sunday to a Reykjavík mass on the state radio station, I wrote this little poem to speculate on God's taste in praise music:

Worship

On Sunday morning in Reykjavík, the radio
plays minor-key hymns in a molasses tempo.
The church sounds empty and probably is.
The praise of God rises like a funeral dirge
into the gray drizzle leaking over Reykjavík.
Whatever you think, the real God is comforted by this.

W. H. Auden liked Sunday morning in Iceland, too. In *Letters from Iceland*—this eccentric and witty travel book describing Iceland in 1936 still provides a good travel guide for the Icelandic habits of mind, even of the country's soul—an invented character, Hetty (who speaks in Auden's voice), says this in a letter: "Not that I am any advocate for religious instruction, which is one of the reasons I like Iceland. Iceland is one of the few places where you don't feel it in the air when it's Sunday." Not on August 24, 1936, and not now either. Auden writes in his own voice from Möðrudalur, "renowned for its home-made ale and a drunken clergyman. The country clergy here are all farmers as well, which brings them in touch with their parishioners, but perhaps rather secularises them. But I fancy that religion has never been very enthusiastic in Iceland." The clergy had sobered up by the time I visited the farm

Möðrudalur in 1979. It's the highest inhabited place in Iceland, four hundred and seventy meters above sea level, a bleak oasis in the middle of a vast black volcanic desert, almost as far from other humans as it is possible to get in Iceland. My great-grandfather Björn Gíslason farmed at the nearest equally bleak farm, Grímsstaðir. His second wife was the granddaughter of the Möðrudalur farmer. A shirttail cousin, Anna Birna, is the farmer's wife at Möðrudalur now.

A Lilliput-sized white concrete church thrusts up its spire in the middle of the black enormity. It was built in 1949 by the farmer Jón Stefánsson, who painted the altarpiece too. It's a peculiar painting. Like most Icelandic artists of his day, Jón was self-taught and painted what pleased him. As I remember, the painting includes Herðubreið (the highest, grandest mountain in sight), a grove of palm trees (there are no trees at all for fifty miles in any direction), and ancient Jews who look a lot like local Icelanders tracking in a line down the mountain. There are four pews in the church, which seat maybe twenty well-fed Icelanders—more than enough for a regular Sunday morning, if there were such a thing. Along with sobering up, the clergy seems to have given up sheep farming, and the priest who occasionally officiates at Möðrudalur probably drives out from Egilsstaðir, the nearest town. When I was there, the church was often the scene of family celebrations—baptisms and confirmations, mostly—and it never came close to holding the assembled horde. No matter. Those who couldn't fit in simply stood outside the open church door, usually in an icy rain, waiting for the service to end and the coffee, *hangikjöt*, and cream-stuffed pancakes to begin.

That's the real function of the Icelandic state Lutheran church: to mark the passages into and out of the world, and to note the major markers along the way. It is one of the bolts holding together the history and culture of the country. Oddly enough, it is even a bolt in the vast, mostly empty landscapes; travelers in Iceland cannot imagine the countryside without the hundreds of modest churches that punctuate it, often on small farmsteads like Möðrudalur—many built of wood, a few of turf, and one or two famous ones of stone. Buildings have never lasted long in Iceland. Most were only driftwood and turf, but some survive intact from the nineteenth century; the oldest, Víðimýri, is a charming turf-and-timber church from 1834. It's in south Skagafjörður, not far from my house. Only two survive from the eighteenth century: the modest cathedral on the government square in the middle of Reykjavík and the miniscule jewel box of a stone cathedral at Hólar, a few kilometers south of Brimnes.

Auden was certainly right in his suspicion that "the church organisation certainly must have been the one thing which civilised the social structure of the settlers." Though Iceland was Christianized in 1000 and Lutheranized in 1550 (with the power of the ax, not a turning of the heart), Christianity, in addition to bringing literacy, education, and a connection to continental cultures, brought about a considerable decline in the number of murders that we find in the world of the sagas.

There have even been a few real Christians among the clergy, foremost among them Guðmundur the Good, bishop of Hólar (the north diocese). Guðmundur Arason (same name, but not the same universal father as the later Bishop Jón) was elected bishop of Hólar in 1201—not appointed by Rome, but rather elected—by the chieftains who hoped to consolidate their power through him, particularly Kolbeinn Tumason, the biggest local potato. Guðmundur dispensed his large church revenues (the Icelanders were required to tithe) "more generously to paupers than Kolbeinn considered wise," says Gunnar Karlsson in his *History of Iceland*. Priests sentenced to outlawry by Kolbeinn were welcomed at Hólar. The quarrels between the two of them will remind students of English history of the struggles between Thomas Becket and King Henry. In this case, Kolbeinn was killed in a fierce battle in 1208, whereupon the chieftains ganged up to expel Guðmundur from Hólar. After being driven out, he was accompanied all over Iceland by the small army of vagrants, paupers, women, and landless farmers whom he had fed and cared for at Hólar. How strange! A Christian feeding the poor!

The Icelanders also loved him for his habit of blessing wells, springs, dangerous roads, and bird cliffs all over the country as he wandered; Jón Hjálmarsson reports that "many place names still bear witness to this practice of the bishop, including the main spring (Gvendarbrunnar) supplying drinking water for Reykjavík." Guðmundur's most famous local blessing here in Skagafjörður is at Drangey, the six-hundred-foot sheer-cliffed island that rises out of the sea six miles away. Since the Middle Ages, Drangey has been a rich source of food: seabirds and seabird eggs. One of the world's famous bird cliffs, it's home to perhaps a million squawking seabirds, who inhabit its walls in layers like a high-rise apartment. To gather the eggs or net the puffins and guillemots, you first scale the cliff straight over the sea, then lash a rope to yourself and a firmly placed stone and swing back and forth, up and down, filling the larder. Ropes fray. The possibilities for instant death are, needless to say, abundant. Drangey has always had a high mortality rate. Guðmundur the Good sailed around the island early in the thirteenth century, doing his best to bless and make it safe. When he reached the northeast side of the island, a giant claw emerged from the cliff, and a harsh, gravelly voice sounded: "Leave some room for us evil ones, too." For the last eight hundred years, egg gatherers have done their best to avoid the northeast cliff.

The Icelanders inherited a fine role model for the practice of Christianity, as well as the theory. A sensible church would have sanctified Guðmundur by now, but Rome always seemed a little suspicious of the faraway Icelanders. After years of wandering with his train of paupers, Guðmundur finally came back to Hólar when he was old, sick, and blind. He died there peacefully in 1237. Ordinary Icelanders, probably even the skeptics and freethinkers, have already sanctified him. Maybe he preached to the birds, too.

Half-lucky in their small size, geographic isolation, and relative poverty, Icelanders have usually escaped the most extreme fanatical paroxysms within Christianity. Some witches were burned in the seventeenth century, all but a few of them men. Their chief offense seems to have been swindling farms from the living. No kinky sexual stuff. While the other Scandinavian countries—particularly Norway—suffered under the pietist revival of Hauge-ism, Iceland was mostly unscathed. Always much more nationalist than theological, the Icelandic church—Catholic or Lutheran—tended to be liberal, tolerant, almost maternal. The clergy were, as Auden thought, more often boozy sheep farmers than dispensers of hellfire and brimstone.

But as with religions generally, Icelandic Lutheranism suffered a sea change in crossing over the Atlantic to the New World. Rev. Páll Þorláksson was among the first immigrants after 1870. He went to seminary—not Icelandic, of course; there never has been one—but in St. Louis among strict, conservative Germans and Haugean Norwegians. He emerged as the first priest for the new immigrants, helping them learn English, find land and a place to settle, and master farming in a new climate with new soil. He was young, earnest, and tireless in his labors to be useful.

The first Icelandic immigrants were grateful to him and liked him as a man. But oh, the theology. . . . He brought from his seminary what we would now call a fundamentalist notion of the literal inerrancy and primacy of scripture, to wit: the Bible in every word is literally true and a literal guide for Christian behavior and thought. He brought also the notion of male primacy in church governance; men and women were separate but unequal and women had no voting (or other) rights in church life. All this he brought to a tribe used to independent thinking and the presence of powerful women—beginning with their mothers. From settlement days, women had enjoyed real power in Iceland, beginning with the famous chieftain, big landowner, and legal advisor Auður the Deep-Minded. Until Christianity arrived, in fact, women enjoyed equal rights to divorce, to own property, and to initiate lawsuits. Erik the Red's daughter, Freyðis, was one of the original business entrepreneurs in the Vinland expeditions and a famously fierce and courageous warrior—though not, by saga evidence, a very pleasant woman. This is not the sort of tradition or history likely to yield easily to the strict and pious certainties of Rev. Páll.

But for the Icelanders—as for every other immigrant group to this day—the wound to the soul caused by the abrupt amputation of language, culture, history, folklore, landscape, and habits of mind and body was too much, too sudden for instant adjustment, for melting immediately into the new pot. The phantom limb still ached and would ache for a long time, sometimes a generation—or two or three—in the New World. The church provided a home, an anchor, a resting place away from the foreign neighbors, the new behemoths of America and Canada. In church, you could live and die in Icelandic, while you had to buy coffee, flour, and your first pig in stumbling English. The Icelanders, lovers of controversy, argument, legal hairsplitting, and large quarrels over small trifles (which in saga days, of course, led to many axes buried in many heads) continued their disputatious, litigious habits in church matters. At least no axes—though the verbal mudslinging might lead one to think they would shortly be sharpened and used.

Rev. Páll became advisor and friend to a young immigrant born at Kirkjuhóll in Skagafjörður. The young man was Stefán Guðmundsson first, in Shawano, Wisconsin, but he became Stephan G. Stephansson, the greatest of the Icelandic emigrant poets and one of the masters of the Icelandic language in the twentieth century. No one in Wisconsin could spell or pronounce his name, with its odd letters and its ordinary Icelandic distinction from either his father's or his mother's name, so he changed it, probably hoping to acclimate. He followed Rev. Páll from Wisconsin, where Stefán was active in Páll's little congregation of lonesome Icelanders, to North Dakota, where the land was easier (not so many damn trees to clear!) and more fertile than that of Shawano. North Dakota also housed a larger Icelandic community and soon had its own churches at Mountain and Gardar.

Thus began the great schism among the Icelanders. Stephan (as he called himself by this time) refused to sign the congregational bylaws for his friend Rev. Páll. Those bylaws included, of course, the inerrancy of scripture and the Apostles' Creed, and the inferior status of women. Though a completely uneducated and penniless farmer, Stephan was a brilliant, well-read, and thoughtful man, an autodidact of the best kind, who insisted on doing his own thinking. His mind was fiercely independent. Worst of all, he refused to lie or dissemble, even to his friends and those who loved him. Páll allowed him not to sign the offending provisions, but for Stephan it was the beginning of the end of his connection not just to Icelandic Lutheranism but to Christianity—in fact, to any sort of revealed religion. Though he'd probably not heard of him yet, he joined the church of Baruch Spinoza, the fellowship of reason. Stephan was a great reader for his entire long life (1853–1927), and his independence in religious and political thought was much influenced by his reading of Emerson, Thoreau, Whitman, Twain, Ingersoll, Paine, Darwin, Marx, and Spencer. Páll Þorláksson died of tuberculosis shortly after his break with Stephan, in 1883, but while Stephan mourned his old friend for his hard work and kindness to his neighbors, he did not mourn his theology.

The Icelandic Lutherans broke apart on these rocky questions, into the Páll-men and the Unitarians, who were closer in thought to the old-country liberal Lutheranism. This rift was accompanied by torrents of debate in the even-then lively Icelandic New-World press, but the religious debate provoked not so much eloquence as gas and wind. The ordinary Icelanders (like those in Minneota, which remained Lutheran and a member of the Icelandic Synod) resolved this question in their usual, historically sanctioned way: by not going to church and doing their best to starve the poor ministers called to baptize and bury them. Stephan G. Stephansson solved the problem by giving up the church completely and moving, a final time, to the wilderness of western Alberta—in Markerville, west of Red Deer— where there was no church at all.

The conservative Norwegian Lutherans had inflicted ruin and exile on one of Stephansson's freethinking heroes, Kristofer Janssen. Janssen came to the Midwest as a circuit-riding Norwegian Lutheran preacher to the huge Norwegian emigrant community. He used his eloquence to offer them the best in nineteenth-century thought and culture: Darwin, Spencer, Emerson, Tolstoy, Goethe, Beethoven—a genuine, independent intellectual life. The Lutherans drummed Janssen out, so he established successful Unitarian societies, some of which survive to this day. Knut Hamsun was his secretary in the late 1880s, though he did not form a high opinion of the emigrant culture or of the church. Janssen was finally ruined by a scandal—an affair with a housemaid—and returned to Copenhagen to die there. When Jón Bjarnason, president of the new Icelandic Synod, attacked Stephan G. (and his freethinking club) in print as a bunch of "uneducated, ignorant farmers" whose object "for the first time in the history of the Icelandic nation was to destroy Christendom," three red flags appeared to goad the bull in Stephansson: he was proud to be a self-educated farmer-intellectual, for centuries the keystone of Iceland's culture; he thought himself not a traitor to Iceland but rather a servant of its language, culture, and tradition; and he wanted to destroy nothing—rather, he thought humans ought to think for themselves, whatever their conclusions.

In Alberta, Stephansson continued to think, read, and debate with his neighbors and in print—meanwhile creating a corpus of eighteen hundred pages of dense, romantic poetry, thought by Icelanders to be a chief glory of their modern literature. He continued, too, the hard labor of wresting a new farm out of the Canadian wilderness. He was always a poor man. At day's end, he returned to his small writing office in his modest farmhouse to make poems through the night. He suffered lifelong insomnia, and called his mammoth collected poems *Andvökur—Wakeful Nights*. Though he gave up any church for the last forty years of his life, he asked his friend in Winnipeg, Rögnvaldur Pétursson, a Unitarian minister, to serve as his literary executor and to bury him. That's probably what churches are for, rightly understood.

The rejuvenation and rightward drift of evangelical Christianity flared up in the New World as if a bellows were being pumped on a dying fire. While the Icelandic Synod didn't quite summon the powers of an inquisition (a phenomenon that—thank Buddha!—missed Iceland), Jón Bjarnason was clearly hunting the hides of heretics to purify the institutional church. Europeans seem to have passed through the worst excesses of organized religion into a state of tolerant, benevolent calm. As an American, I can suggest that they have a surprise coming—and probably not a pleasant one. The new immigration will certainly fuel revivals of faith all over the old continent—not Catholics, Lutherans, Calvinists, and Anglicans, but rather Muslims, conservative Christians, Hindus, and Sikhs (it's hard to imagine fanatical Buddhists and Taoists).

The Icelandic Synod of the Lutheran Church is now dead—only a historical blip, amalgamated first with the Swedes and now finally assimilated into the big, new corporate synod that includes all the old ethnicities and some surprising new ones. As synods go, it is mostly kind and tolerant, a little sleepy, a true ghost of the old-country Icelanders rather than the narrow Haugean revivals of the past. Still not many tambourines, but an electric-guitar mass here and there as bait to get the young and hip back into the pews. It won't work. The new wave of religious frenzy in America is either Pentecostal and Fundamentalist or suburban enclaves of vast, nondenominational warehouse congregations. But it's there, healthy and alive, and it plays an enormous and influential role in American public life and discourse. Stephan G. Stephansson could not be elected dogcatcher in the United States at the moment. Nor could Baruch Spinoza, if anyone would even take the trouble to read him.

I was eleven years old and a pupil at country school, Yellow Medicine County District 90, when the phrase "under God" was added to the Pledge of Allegiance. This was, after all, the Cold War, and we had a mission to defend America and

Christianity from the godless Communists. Senator McCarthy (and millions of others) said so. "Under God" would help to remind us of our job—or mission—as would the Pledge itself.

I remember the old Icelanders in the neighborhood who assembled to slurp coffee from their saucers in my parents' kitchen. They disdained this publicly sanctioned religious bullying. "Under what god? Whose? What has god got to do with the state?" I don't imagine they were very happy about the patriotic bullying either—a pledge of allegiance, indeed! But Americans have always loved demanding loyalty oaths of their neighbors, a civil form of reciting the Apostles' Creed in church. We're just checking to see that you're really one of us. Historians call this American phenomenon "civil religion," but I think it's large enough to include religions of all variety—even the Lutherans.

I cannot remember the last time an American president closed a speech without demanding that God Bless America. They all said it: Johnson, Nixon, the Bushes, and Clinton. In fact, the last presidential candidate to have refrained from saying it was probably Eugene McCarthy, an actual practicing Catholic who knew a thing or two about both theology and public life, and the differences between them.

It was the Apostles' Creed that finally tripped up Stephan G. Stephansson. Rev. Páll asked him to sign a paper indicating that he subscribed to all of its assertions. He couldn't do that, he said, because he was still thinking about them, slowly and carefully. There was a lot to examine in that small paragraph. He must have understood then that he was essentially finished as a churchman in America—or, for that matter, in Canada. As an Icelander, he would probably have survived at home as a member of the state church, then and now. Who in Iceland would have asked him to testify as to his opinions or his thinking? Not the priest, not the bishop, and certainly not his neighbors. Like most Icelanders, Stephansson thoroughly enjoyed disputing questions of religion (or any other subject), trying on first one side of an issue and then the other, in order to see how the arguments worked, what surprising evidence might be summoned in the course of debate.

Auden found the same habit in Icelanders in 1936. He must have just discovered the *Saga of the Faroe Islanders*, translated for the first time into English and published by Muriel Press in 1864, but reissued in London in 1934.

Thora asked him what teaching his foster-father had given him on Holy Writ. Sigmund said he had learnt his paternoster and creed. Thora said—I would like to hear it! On which he sang his paternoster, as she thought, pretty well. But Sigmund's creed ran thus—

Given to us are angels good,
Without them go I ne'er a foot;
Where'er I am, where'er I fare
Five angels follow everywhere.
Paltering prayer, if so I be,
To Christ they bear them presently:
Psalms, too, seven can I sing—
Have mercy on me, God my King.

At this moment Thrand comes into the room and asks what they are talking about. Thora answers and says her son has been rehearsing the Christian knowledge he had taught him. But the creed seems to be wrong! "Ah!" said Thrand, "Christ, you know, had twelve disciples or more, and each of them had his own credo. Now I have my credo, and you have the credo you have been taught; there are many credos, and they may be right without being exactly the same." And with that the conversation ended.

I asked the new bishop of Hólar, Jón Aðalsteinn Baldvinsson, about that story. Yes, he thought the story an accurate description of the way Icelanders think, the way they understand their relationship to the church. All the creeds may be right without being alike. I subscribe to this notion myself. As a matter of fact, I am still a member in good standing of St. Paul's Icelandic Lutheran Church in Minneota, now a ghostly remnant of the congregation of my boyhood—shrunken in size and elderly, but still alive. As Rev. Jón suspected, no one has ever asked me what I believe about the creed: the triune God, the resurrection, the Eucharist, and the atonement. It's none of your business what I believe, or if I believe, nor is it the church's business. I'd guess that a large majority of modern Icelanders would subscribe to the previous sentence—though without admitting that they agree with it. That's none of my business. My business is tolerance, kindness, charity, and proper voice leading—in Bach chorales, for example.

THE HOME OF POETRY

Where does poetry live? On a poor, remote farm on an arctic fjord on an equally remote island in the middle of a cold ocean? Or on a pig-fragrant farm on an eroded small hill at the navel of North America, the vast trackless prairie, a half day's drive from any city? Are these places we expect poetry—literature— to be born and to flourish in the interior lives of their inhabitants? In fact, there is no "likely" place for poetry to arrive. It arrives where it pleases, for reasons of its own. From which corner of the brain or soul does the craving for language made into music arise in human beings? We don't know; we shall never know. We can gather, based on history and experience, that it is not connected to money, higher education, social position, government programs, piety, respectability, or even good manners. To what, then, is it connected? In truth, it is attached to the tail of a mystery that cannot be unraveled.

The farm on the fjord is, of course, in Iceland, halfway between Europe and North America. For the first thousand years of its history (from 874 to 1874 and after), it existed without towns, roads, libraries, or schools, its small population scattered on isolated farms, most in a condition of poverty of unchallenged meanness. In the absence of any timber, most buildings here—houses, churches, barns—were constructed of lumps of turf and a bit of driftwood, roofed with grass in the summer and snow drifts in the long winter. These houses were usually small, unheated, and thus eternally damp and cold, foul-smelling on account of too many unwashed bodies and too many unemptied chamber pots, and filled with sour, half-rotten food, little light, and no ventilation at all. The Icelanders preserve a few of them as museums and reminders of their past, but they have all been cleaned and restored, and they are inhabited for only a few hours of the summer day by guides and ticket takers. The animals and the odorous chamber pots are elsewhere. You may choose to visit them if you like. Since I am a descendant of their inhabitants, I happily stay clear of them. Indeed, the very thought of them depresses me.

Yet in those foul hovels on this cold, lonesome island, poetry, history, and tales were generated abundantly in the course of those one thousand years. You may know of the Sagas, the Eddic poems, and the histories of Snorri Sturluson. They have all entered world literature with just reputation and renown. But you have almost certainly never heard of Jón Espólín (1769–1836), the incompetent sheriff of Skagafjörður, who wrote, among other lengthy works, a mammoth twelve-volume yearbook of Icelandic history from 1300 to 1830, which included a 117-page index of personal names. Or of Jón Þorláksson (1744–1819), the farmer-priest from Bægisá close by in the next county, who spent a few winters translating *Paradise Lost* into Icelandic. Among Icelanders, this glorious achievement is often said to equal, or even exceed, the sublime grandeur of the original. He also translated Pope, Klopstock from the German, and the Psalms into Icelandic verse forms. In addition, that is, to composing a thousand pages of his own highly regarded poetry.

Nor have you likely heard of Gísli Konráðsson (1787–1877), who farmed at Húsabakki, about twenty-five miles south of my house in Brimnes. Among other projects, Gísli translated Sir Walter Scott's compendious biography of Napoleon from Danish into Icelandic, composed a lengthy autobiography with a vast index of names, and completed Jón Espólín's first draft of the *Húnvetninga Saga*—nine hundred printed pages with a one hundred and fifty page index—a history of the next county west. Gísli's great reputation, however, was as a poet. Indeed, his greatest talent was for the Icelanders' favorite four-line verses, the *lausa vísa*, which he was said to compose at the speed of normal speech. Poetry seemed an animal living, always awake, inside a human brain, in continual readiness. But his magnum opus is a 603-stanza history of the world, from its beginnings to the date of the poem's composition in the early 1850s. Beginning with Adam and Eve, this extraordinary work covers the birth of Christ and the beginnings of the Christian age, the five centuries of the Dark Ages that preceeded the discovery of Iceland in 874, the first 800 years of Iceland's history (in the context of that of the rest of the world, of course), and finally the 150 years of the modern world, ending with the California gold rush and the Paris revolt of 1848. Viðar Hreinsson, a literary scholar and historian of no small reputation, assures me that it is fine work, elegantly composed in rhymed and alliterated quatrains, and adorned throughout with great learning and touches of wit. All this accomplished while Gísli was otherwise engaged as a farmer at Húsabakki, cutting hay, milking cows, tending a large herd of sheep, and catching and salting fish from the big glacial river that flows through the farm!

Viðar Hreinsson tells a wonderful story that illuminates Gísli's life and character. Until the mid-twentieth century, Icelandic farms were mostly self-sufficient, but the farmers were compelled to trade for what could not be gathered in Iceland. Gísli once sent his hired man off to the Danish store, a day's ride away, to shop for necessities: coffee, flour, sugar, nails, fish hooks, and for Gísli a ream of paper. Tempted to enjoy a little drink and sociability on his shopping trip, the farmhand returned a day late, whereupon he presented himself to Gísli. Gísli inquired as to how the trip had gone. The farmhand replied that he had successfully bargained for everything: coffee, flour, and sundries. "But where's my ream of paper?" asked Gísli. "Damn," said the farm hand. "I'm afraid I forgot it." "That is a shame," said Gísli. "A wasted trip."

Recently I drove to Húsabakki with my neighbor Hallgrímur, to see where Gísli lived and worked one-hundred-and-fifty years ago. The house and barn are newer, of course, but the named farm site remains the same. There is a one-lane dirt road that turns inland about eight miles south of the fjord, and winds across vast flat boggy meadows for four or five miles, over an old wooden bridge, then along a glacial outwash river. The meadows gleamed with cottongrass, buttercups, and dandelions in the bright arctic noonday sun, the sky piercing blue. Golden plovers flitted along the road, a half-dozen ravens flew low, looking for dinner, countless redshanks hooted in chorus, and ring-necked plovers ran out in front of the car, posing on the road to distract us from their eggs or chicks. Hallgrímur and I admired this fertile, watery, almost-hidden place. I imagined Gísli, finally in possession of his fresh ream, bringing his astounding skills to bear on the intricate quatrains describing the California gold rush, so far from boggy Húsabakki.

After our trip, an Icelandic family in town for the weekend came to call at Brimnes: father, mother, and a very clever twelve-year-old son. I described my trip to Húsabakki, and the remarkable facts of Gísli's literary labors. Kjartan looked puzzled. He copied by hand all those pages of Napolean? Why didn't he just scan them? I realized with a shudder that at sixty-three I was closer to Gísli's world than to Kjartan's—which was farther from my life and mind than the California gold rush—or from the compulsive scribbling that happened on an isolated Icelandic farm. Another world has arrived, victorious, and I hardly noticed its advent. It wins, certainly, but with what consequence for human beings?

What should one call this odd but wonderful Icelandic tradition of farmer-intellectuals, poets, and historians? I choose to call it the Line of Gísli, though a multitude of other names could be summoned. Indeed, it is a tradition that continues today all over this island, often in obscure rural places, but even in newly urban Reykjavík. And it is wonderfully alive in the person of my neighbor, Kristján Árnason.

I first met Kristján at Lónkot, an ancient farm now turned summer resort with restaurant, bar, guest rooms, campsites, and a mammoth green tent used for culture, commerce, craft shows, and family reunions. Only a few kilometers north of my house, it sits elegantly beside the fjord, with a commanding view of islands, mountains, and the water. One July afternoon, I went for an afternoon of readings and music in the big green tent, what the Icelanders call a *listahátíd*. A skilled pianist played a half hour of old plums: Ravel's "Pavane," Debussy's "Clair de Lune," the Chopin Nocturne, the Rachmaninoff Prelude; a gorgeous mezzo sang Schubert, Wolf, and romantic Icelandic songs; and then finally Einar Már Guðmundsson, Iceland's best-selling and most beloved novelist, read from a book I knew in English, and so could follow Einar's Icelandic. Einar and I had been friendly for a good while, so I looked forward to seeing him.

The crowd in the green tent sat in bleachers facing each other while Einar read from the middle dais. Einar had just won a Nordic Council Prize for the best Scandinavian novel of the year and was the current toast of the literary north. He is a blond, handsome, youthful-looking fellow with deep-set eyes and an unpretentious manner. He began his literary career as a poet and started the reading with a few of his best-loved poems. I sat watching the audience on the other side react to these poems that most of them probably knew, some even by heart. One face caught my attention: an older man, almost gray, a fine-featured, sensitive face that was almost continually in motion, his hands and shoulders rising and falling involuntarily, animated by what appeared to be an interior electrical charge. Parkinson's, I assumed, a disease that ravages Icelanders in what are probably greater than normal numbers.

When Einar finished to hearty applause, the crowd adjourned to the Lónkot restaurant for the essential afternoon coffee and cream cakes. I found Einar huddled over a thick pile of paper with the old gentleman I'd observed during the reading. "Meet your neighbor, Kristján Árnason, the poet. Why don't you read these and give Kristján some advice on his English poems?" Kristján and I shook hands, and I sat down with my coffee and forty or fifty pages of English verse. English? Here we were in northern Iceland, far from bilingual Reykjavík, and I was reading the English poems of a local carpenter and farmer. The stack of Icelandic poems that faced Einar was far thicker, a few hundred deep. I discovered later that there was also a stack of Danish poems, should any wandering Danes have chanced to come by. The English poems were partly awkward imitations of Keats, Shelley, Burns, etc., rhymed, romantic stanzas in praise of the beauty of nature and (more heartfelt) of lovely girls. But Kristján practiced satiric limericks, too, and with considerable wit and skill. The shenanigans of Bill and Monica were the subject of several of my favorites.

During the course of our conversations, Kristján revealed himself to be an unapologetic lefty and peacenik, no fancier of American foreign policy and economic bullying. We chatted awhile, the beginning of a friendship. He was indeed my close neighbor, with a little house and property on the next farm, Skálá, a few miles north of Hofsós. He had lived and worked mostly as a carpenter and a skilled cabinetmaker. In fact, he'd been one of the carpenters on the handsome bar and restaurant where we now sat sipping coffee. His slightly accented English was elegant, correct, and fluent. Where had he learned it? He'd never gone past grammar school from the farm in Borgarfjördur in west Iceland where he was born on March 14, 1929. He'd read in English, as so many Icelanders do, then spent several years working at the NATO base at Keflavík, where the conversations of soldiers cemented his idiomatic English. Danish was the common second language of Icelanders in his youth, difficult for an Icelander to pronounce but simple to read. He had moved from his native district to the north of Skagafjörður in 1975 to do a carpentry job at Skálá. He liked the feel of the neighborhood, found plenty of work, and stayed.

Kristján and I became friends after this first meeting. He'd drive his old Volvo into Hofsós or I'd drive out to the schoolhouse that he'd remodeled into a cozy apartment and a spacious workshop for his woodworking machinery and supplies. Mr. Parkinson's, as he called his disease, had come to call on him in 1990, so he'd given up full-time carpentry. Instead, he exercised his artistic side by making beautiful wooden bowls, statues, objets d'art, wooden toys for the Skálá children—who adored the old bachelor and nicknamed him Grandpa Kiddi— and writing poetry, of course. He'd begun to write occasional poetry at the age of fifteen, still on the farm. At first versifying was a hobby, an amusement (one practiced by an astonishing number of Icelanders), but as Kristján once said in a newspaper interview, "Poetry always slept within me." It broke out in full force in his maturity. By 2001, he confessed to having over a thousand poems in his computer, though if he doesn't like them after he's let them age awhile and then tried to improve them, he throws them away. Fortunately, some survive.

By 2007, he has certainly written a great many more. He reminisced that his father, the farmer Árni Kristjánsson, "did not write poetry, but he knew a terrific amount by heart and he taught me. He was always quoting poetry to me."

After he was diagnosed with Parkinson's, Kristján began pruning and assembling his work for a book, which he printed himself and sold by subscription, a common practice in Iceland. Almost every Icelander's great dream is to see his name on a book spine. His first book, *Fjöllin sál og ásynd eiga (The Mountains Have Both Soul and Face)*, appeared in 1994. When I met Kristján in 1998, he was assembling work for his second book: *Mér finnst gott að hafa verið til (I Find It Good to Have Lived, or I Like Being Alive)*, 112 poems and quatrains (an epigrammatic form the Icelanders call *stökur*). Kristján's second book appeared in 2001. In English, Kristján experiments with free verse, even with prose poems, but in Icelandic he calls himself "a pretty old-fashioned poet. I keep to the form and want my poems to follow the rules." The title of his second book came from a funeral poem he wrote before a heart-bypass operation. He said in 2001, "I'm far from thoughts of giving up and I've not stopped writing poetry. I'll carry on for a while yet."

And carry on he does, though the advance of Parkinson's drove him out of the wonderful nest he'd planned for his old age and to the old people's home in Sauðárkrókur, the county town of Skagafjörður, twenty miles away. It is a kindly place, built on a small hill overlooking the fjord and mountains, with views out the big glass windows that would elsewhere adorn a luxury hotel. Kristján lives in a private room with tables for his computer and writing desk and shelves for his books and bric-a-brac. For a while his woodworking tools were in the basement, and he could visit them when he felt strong enough to make his beautiful layered bowls of multicolored wood. For a while, too, friends drove him the hundred and twenty miles back to his house for an afternoon, sometimes to gather arctic berries on his small property, sometimes to admire the progress of a tiny grove of trees he'd planted and tended in this treeless place. But Parkinson's is relentless. He is now very weak and bound to his room, though he still moves to his computer to write and revise. He has even written the poem he intends to be sung at his funeral. His voice has almost disappeared, making conversation close to impossible in either Icelandic or English. When I see him now, I give him news of my literary progress, and he hands me new poems. My Icelandic is in no way good enough to judge, but Icelanders assure me that his work is skillfully, even elegantly, made, full of tender romantic imagery, true emotion, and also true wit and thought. Whatever happens to the future of poetry in this age of digital media, Kristján has served his art faithfully for over sixty years, and will continue to do so until he has need for his funeral song.

Like most of the old Icelandic poets, Kristján is skilled at occasional verse, for birthdays, births, marriages, and deaths. In 2003, I asked him if he might like to write a quatrain congratulating a friend of my long-dead grandmother in America who was about to turn a healthy one hundred. Of course, he said, and produced an elegant little poem in English for Sophia, who, of course, didn't read Icelandic.

Here are a few samples of Kristján's work; the first two quatrains are a genre Stökur in Icelandic, small quick poems in an intricate, strict pattern.

Konan sem ég mætti áðan

Brjóstin vagga sem blóm á stilki,
Bugður líkamans fullkomnar.

Hörundið undir svörtu silki
Sexinu geislar alls staðar.

The Woman Who Passed a Moment Ago

Breasts swaying like flowers on a stalk,
Curves of the body perfect.
Skin covered with black silk
. Radiating sensuality.

Á fjöllum

Á fjöllum vindasveipur sefur,
Sjávarkindur veðrið ræða.
Mittislinda mjúkum vefur
Um miðja tinda skýjaslæða.

In the Mountains

In the mountains a current of wind is sleeping,
Sheep by the sea discuss the weather.
A curtain of clouds wraps a soft cummerbund
Around the middle of the peaks.

All Icelandic words have primary syllable stress. Lines one and three use internal alliteration; the lines rhyme ABAB. Probably half the population of Iceland can spontaneously improvise such a quatrain on almost any subject, in satire or praise. A famous one reads forward as praise, the same words backward as insult. It's a word game, of course, largely possible because of the highly inflected grammatical structure of Icelandic. But it is, in any case, a pleasure for both maker and audience, the pleasure of language made sharply.

The second poem, on the other hand, is not a word game. It's a delicate nocturne made by a man of great sensitivity, an old romantic.

Haust

Á bleiku laufi daggardropar glitra
er draumsins óður snýst í vökulag.
Fölir geislar feimnislega titra
er fikra sig um ungan nakinn dag.
Og dagur rís af beði blíðrar nætur,
breiðir sér á herða dökkan feld,
hlakkar til að starfa, fara á fætur
og falla í dökka arma næsta kveld.

Autumn

Dewdrops glitter on pink leaves
when the dreaming ode changes to a waking song.
The shyly trembling pale sun rays
feel their way into the young naked day.
The day rises from its gentle night bed,
donning its dark cloak about its shoulders.
Time to start glad work, rise to your feet,
then sink into the evening's dark arms.

Kristján's devotion to his art, made without ambition or pretense but rather from love and necessity, has moved me more than once to write about him. Not necessarily because he is peculiar—he isn't, at least not in Iceland—but rather because he represents some core of sanity, if not grandeur, in Icelandic culture and in human beings at large. Poetry is what we do for each other to earn the honor of being human.

The Palestine Flag in Iceland

The old poet with Parkinson's
keeps a Palestine flag on his desk
in the nursing home, To remind him
of the suffering of others, he says.
When Parkinson's steals his voice,
he folds one paper airplane after another,
flying them up and down the hall
to amuse the nurses—and himself.
These planes carry neither messages nor bombs,
but unlike the history of human failure
they are endlessly recyclable.
Outside the big nursing home windows
Iceland stretches off to the horizon,
mountain, sea, town, bombed
only by lava and rain.

Robert Bly had it right when he said:

The hermit said: "Because the world is mad,
The only way through the world is to learn
The arts and double the madness. Are you listening?"

We Americans have Walt Whitman as an embodiment of
this working-class devotion to making art for a whole community, and, though he asked us to become a great audience
fit for great poems, we have largely failed to do so. His humane ideas about war, tolerance, bodily joy, and the failures in
national life seem as ignored now as they were in his lifetime.
Leaves of Grass was Whitman's paper airplane that he folded
and flew toward us time after time as he doubled the madness.

The airplane always fell to earth, but he always, as Kristján did, formed it again to have another try.

I take heart, as an American, from the life of this now-frail man who has spent sixty years trying to tune our ears to hear the music of the universe as it sounds inward, as Bach, for instance, sounded it in tones. Kristján has long been listening. And I'm keeping my ears peeled.

FOG

I bought Brimnes in 1998, in a hopeful spirit—for my personal life, at least, if not for the public life around me—and quickly, completely surrendered to the charm, grandeur, and batty sweetness of the place. Now I spend summers filling notebook after notebook with poems and reflections. And when, around the beginning of August, the eternal daylight begins to fade, the harbor lights come on before midnight, and the birds head south en masse, I must prepare to cross back over the Atlantic: to heat, mosquitoes, teaching, the news on public radio, the blue half of my neighbors paralyzed and whining, the red half anesthetized by greed, Jesus, and patriotic gore. But for three months each year, I am completely, stupidly happy, staring out the big windows at these marvelous mountains, the kaleidoscope colors of the sea, the gallery of clouds and weather that moves past, an opera of light and bird cries. I wait for the knocks on the door—there is no phone—to see what pleasures will arrive: old friends, new friends, musicians, fishermen, children to pilfer chocolate and teach me a few words of Icelandic, offers for bizarre trips into the countryside, sheep's-head dinners, cocktails on the next deck uphill, visitors from Australia. And then at least an hour of daily exercise at the piano: one summer Scarlatti; one, nothing but French music—Couperin, Fauré, Debussy; one, Scriabin; one, Hindemith, and all of these punctuated with hours of Bach and Haydn.

However, while my summers continue to be mostly sane and often idyllic, the world has not always cooperated. The eerie

phony election of 2000; the terrorist attack of 2001; the bru-
tal and ignorant response to that brutality in 2002, accompanied by the rattling snare drums of war; the invasion of Iraq in
2003—the stupidest act ever committed by the United States
(and like others, we've done some doozies); and then the 2004
elections, proof of a paralyzed national brain and permanently
off-duty media.

Each of the few summers since, I have been back in front of
the windows at Brimnes, resuming my scribble—but this past
year all was changed. Next time someone tells you to be cheerful about the weather, or that it makes no difference to human
psychology, you may with my glad dispensation tell them to go
to hell. Indeed, weather is everything. Only the dead experience no weather.

This last summer has been white, blank almost from beginning till now, the end of July. I arrived here in May to a howling
blizzard, a genuine, ferocious three-day blow with horizontal
snow, gale-force winds, ten-foot drifts, and buried bird eggs.
For two weeks after the blizzard, cold rain fell, while the sea
turned violent and noisy in the southwest wind. On June 11,
Tindastóll disappeared. It snowed into the fog on June 12. The
sky cleared for half a day June 13, then closed again. It opened
a little every couple of days until July 6, when the shade went
down for good. For twenty-two days (with eight and a half
hours of reprieve) we lived in an invisible white world—no
texture, no color, no depth, no height, no sky, no earth, and, of
course, no dark at this season, so no day and no night, just that
pale, milky, impenetrable scrim.

I can assure you that three or four weeks of blank weath-
erlessness has psychological implications for human beings.
Without the piano—only Bach can cut through this—and a
little whiskey to warm the innards, I would probably now be an
ax murderer or a straitjacketable maniac. In consequence, the

tone shifts in the prose. For years my next-door neighbor, the wise Hallgrímur, listened to my descriptions of Iceland, then chided me: "Too damn much whipped cream and jam. You think Iceland saner, smarter than other places. It's not. We're just ordinary human scoundrels and fools." I suppose, then, that life in the white fog drained out a shovelful or two of whipped cream.

The Icelanders suffer their own interior fog at the moment. It muddles their view of themselves and the world. Mostly because of poverty and isolation, Iceland missed the Renaissance, the Reformation (it arrived at sword point from Denmark), the Enlightenment, and the Industrial Revolution—thus most of the last eight hundred years. Icelandic society proceeded directly from the Middle Ages to the cell phone, the airplane, and the Internet. Until twenty years ago, the country had hardly a passable highway, and it still has no railroads (Icelanders who don't travel have never seen a train), nor any ghosts of obsolete, moldering factories. In fact, there were no factories at all here until an aluminum smelter arrived (via the Swiss) in 1969.

Iceland had cheap electricity to offer (hydropower), and aluminum smelting requires vast amounts of it. The temptation to make "deals" with kindly corporate behemoths like Alcan and Alcoa proved irresistible to the Icelanders, and soon smelters will blossom all over the country, giving the volcanic wilderness a new look and feel. To make electricity, you dam rivers, flood canyons, remodel nature to your own commercial ends. There's a lot of "nature" in Iceland: grand, bleak, eerie, uninhabited (probably uninhabitable) volcanic deserts; glacial detritus bullying its way to the sea through huge, boggy marshes. That wilderness is home to wild reindeer, falcons, and eagles, and it provides nesting grounds for a multitude of other birds. It is like nowhere else on earth, and if the Icelanders keep selling it off to make beer cans for global conglomerates with souls and senses of honor the size of fleas, it will indeed exist nowhere at all except in photographs and memory.

In short, the Icelanders are selling their dreamland to the aluminum companies, and for a mess of pottage. Aluminum is now three thousand dollars a ton, but what rises falls. At fifteen hundred a ton, Alcoa will demand cheaper electricity or else close the smelter. Unemployment... discontent... bankruptcy... and naturally, the bill for the giant engineering project—tunnels, reservoirs, generators—will be left for the Icelandic taxpayer. And it will leave them a ruined, deflowered landscape to boot.

All of which is to say that the Icelanders are giving up their only real patrimony—the emptiness and wisdom of nature—for money. Befogged by words like *jobs, progress, development, tax base,* and *opportunity,* they are damming up, tunneling, gouging, and dynamiting several hundred square miles of their country—wilderness, even—for money. They have cut out part of the lungs of the hydrological systems by which nature—their country—breathes. And oddly enough, they have not been compensated fairly in the process. You never are when you deal with the hooded suit. Americans know this because it's usually an American suit these days, but money carries no real passport. It loves nothing but more of itself. Under the hood is a skull with golden teeth. It smiles. You've already signed, so now the second act can begin. Bring up the fog!

A key component of this grand project will be a giant dam at Kárahnjúkur in the wilds of east Iceland. It will create a forty-square-mile lake out of the black canyon of the Jökulsá (Glacier River), which will generate the mammoth amount of electricity needed to fuel the new aluminum smelter being built on an east-coast fjord. The Kárahnjúkur dam and smelter project is, of course, a disaster, and a senseless one at that, but under the eloquent goading of writers, scientists, even an enlightened journalist or two, Icelanders are trying to reopen the debate on whether it should have been started at all and whether it should continue. Too late. Americans seem to be the bringers of all such bad news these days. Once you have done something so completely idiotic as to dam the Icelandic highlands, or to invade Iraq, you are going to be there, and for a long time. It is going to cost you enormous quantities of blood and money, and it may well ruin your international reputation and sink your sense of honor. All this from false evidence, political posturing and dissembling, and, awful though it is to think, profiteering. "Show me who is making a profit, and I'll show you who started the war," said Henry Ford during World War I. As something of a profiteer himself, Henry would have known.

All this happened in Iceland as with us: with minimal real public debate, no national circulation of accurate or contrary information, and no respected national voices with the courage to say a loud no. (To be precise, there was one in America— Paul Wellstone, the Senator from Minnesota, but he died too soon, and strangely.) So with the Icelanders, though less blood will be spilt by the dam and smelter. If Icelanders imagine they own enough empty nature to fool around with for the possibility of quick profit, they should remember what their country looked like a thousand-odd years ago when the settlers arrived: birch forests everywhere, uneroded hills and ravines, a sea and rivers teeming with fish stocks that looked inexhaustible—but weren't.

When W. H. Auden made a nostalgic return to Iceland in the mid-sixties, after thirty years' absence, he found the light still

magical, but a new prosperity, then from fish catches, alter-
ing the face of Iceland. Many hundreds of years' experience of
poverty had not weakened what Auden loved: the "only truly
classless society" (maybe true, maybe not), the resilience of a
homegrown literary culture that valued narrative and versifying skill, and a deep and essential decency and kindness of
character. Auden found these traits still alive in the sixties, but
he worried. The Icelanders had proved their genius at surviving poverty with spirits intact, but what might prosperity do
to them? In the sixties, Auden thought them "still not vulgar,
not yet. . . ."

Unfortunately, the trend is moving in the wrong direction.
The mania for aluminum smelters, gigantic dams, and electric
generators—as at Kárahnjúkur—grows daily. Heavy industry
is in the air: proposals for more aluminum, oil depots, refiner-
ies, and new factories in the wilderness. The real estate market
has gone berserk, with houses, farms, any plot of land bloating
in value five or six times in a few years, and sometimes even
doubling or tripling in a single year. The newspapers swell
to twice their size with ads for *fasteignair*. Summerhouses
go for twenty million krónur ($250-300,000) or much more.
Reykjavík—indeed, much of the country—is jammed with
huge, expensive vehicles—Land Cruisers, SUVs, Mercedes,
Lexus—despite ruinous gas prices and much public debate
about carbon emissions. New housing estates and high-rises
metastasize on every empty inch of undeveloped ground in
the suburbs. Throw in a few new giant enclosed shopping
malls, and dozens of separate big-box retail behemoths for dry
goods, food, home-repair supplies, and furniture. Reykjavík
is no longer a small city surrounded by three or four small
towns or villages. Whatever the charter or the signs say, it
is a single pulsing metropolis that has swallowed its neighbors. It now boasts true rush-hour traffic jams, six lanes of a

slowly inching parking lot. As pulsing urban centers go, it is high priced and, Iceland being small, houses probably three-quarters of the national population. That's not Manhattan or Shanghai or São Paulo, but it's at least a young cousin with a family resemblance.

In the meantime, the bottom has dropped out of ordinary blue-collar working life. Jobs in farming, fishing, or fish processing have disappeared all over Iceland. Farms drop one after the other like heads thudding into a basket in the French Revolution. That's a gruesome metaphor, but nonetheless true. Icelanders survived as farmers—mostly of sheep, cows, and attendant hay—for over a thousand years of their history. That is coming to an end. Most farmers here are over sixty, while the children are in faraway Reykjavík at their computers, cashing in on the new urban prosperity. What will become of the grand old farmer-intellectual culture in the new Internet and venture capital age? No one knows yet, but the signs for its survival are not good.

The signs may be even worse for the fishermen. The local word is that cod stocks are seriously depleted, along with other commercial catches such as haddock and halibut. I can explain the system of fish "quotas" neither to you nor to myself—nor can most Icelanders. Suffice it to say that without a quota, there's no point fishing, and quotas—forbiddingly expensive to acquire—are like stocks, bonds, or real estate. They belong not to beslickered fishermen on a greasy boat deck on a rolling sea, but rather to investors who can afford to acquire and profit from them. Quotas have mostly disappeared from small fishing towns around the coast, with many going to Reykjavík, and some to Akureyri in the north. The ships that harvest the fish are large, expensive, high-tech trawlers that scrape the ocean floor and scoop up in their nets everything they find— by the ton, though only some will be salable under quota.

Hofsós, with its fine and well-maintained harbor, has no quota, so it's a quiet place these days. Most boats are beached in a field above the river. The fish plant, once a freezing house, then for a few years a fish-salting station, and last year a hard-fish works, stands empty this year. The same story appears almost daily in the Icelandic press: yet another down-on-its-luck fishing village.

All this brings to mind the old cliché "the stink of money." I first heard it, I suppose, from my father. When the wind blew from the east, the fragrance of the pig barn entered my mother's domain without her permission, causing sarcastic complaints. "The stink of money," my father said. "That's what we eat." My friend John Rezmerski, who grew up in an odorous pulp-mill town in Pennsylvania, heard the same phrase from his father. It means, of course, that making money—getting rich, though neither John's nor my father did—is not a pretty business. George Bernard Shaw's Captain Shotover in *Heartbreak House*, when asked to devise a profitable invention to save his impecunious relatives, agrees to do so but demands, "Give me deeper darkness; money is not made in the light." When vast fortunes accumulate, as they recently have in Iceland, and a whole culture seems to join in the money grab, it does not give off a good odor. It cannot, by its very nature, any more than a pig lot or a pulp mill can. Auden certainly would have caught the whiff.

So that's the news from Iceland these days, mixed as news usually is—of venality, foolishness, greed, and idealism, intelligence, and humor. As I come to a close, the fog has thickened and deepened. You will have to take it on faith that there really is a Tindastóll and an ocean out there; but how much of our life do we take on faith in the invisible—or even the imaginary? I have expressed my grief here for the behavior of my country through almost all my adult life, now over forty years. Not all its behavior, of course; it has partly grown up with civil rights, women's rights (though not enough yet of either), and a decent-though-not-perfect system of education—after all, a farm boy like me could get one, then pass on a little of it teaching. But we must, as a country, go cold turkey on war, xenophobia, the remodeling of nature for commerce, and religious enthusiasm that veers toward fanaticism. And above all, we must curb greed. Don't hold your breath waiting for progress. I've been waiting a long time. When I look west, over the fog bank, the mountain, Greenland, Canada, to my life in Minneota, I see still more fog, but interior fog.

An image from *The New York Times* on Sunday, August 5, 2001 has haunted me for these five years during which I have reflected upon the world out the windows of Brimnes. I saved the front-page color photograph with this caption: "President Bush joined members of his cabinet in prayer at the beginning of a meeting on Friday afternoon." They are all lined up, seated at a table littered with coffee cups and Coke glasses, hands piously folded, heads bowed, in unison: Cheney, Powell, Bush, Rumsfeld, and Tenet. Karl Rove sits behind them, equally pious. What are they praying for? To whom? For whom? For the camera, obviously; this is a posed picture. Somebody invited *The New York Times* to take this photograph. Just a month before 9/11. Had no one in this room—or in America—read Christ's parable of the Pharisee? Go into your closet and pray, to speak to God in solitude, not to make a noisy spectacle of yourself before men. Maybe not. Reading is not in fashion these days. But this picture still haunts me. The fog around it is dark indeed.

So don't come to the windows of Brimnes to pray—instead, lift your head to peer about, even into the heart of the fog. Take it all in: grandeur, foolishness, the whole lot. And then: praise something. Sing. Maybe Bach, to lift the fog.

END NOTES

ETHEREAL FRIENDS

41: Snorri Sturluson, *The Prose Edda*, trans. Jean Young (Berkeley and Los Angeles: University of California Press, 1964), 63–64.

42: Seamus Heaney, trans., *Beowulf* (New York: Farrar, Straus and Giroux, 2000), lines 3023–3027.

43: Davíð Stefánsson, "Krummi," trans. Wincie Jóhannsdottir, John Rezmerski, and Bill Holm.

59: D.H. Lawrence, "Piano," *The Complete Poems of D.H. Lawrence*, ed. Vivian de Sola Pinto and Warren Roberts (New York: Penguin Books, 1971), 148.

60: Gerard Manley Hopkins, *The Poems of Gerard Manley Hopkins*, ed. W.H. Gardner and N.H. Mackenzie, 4th ed. (London: Oxford University Press, 1967), 69.

ELVES OUT THE WINDOWS

64: Jón Arnason, comp., *Icelandic Legends*, trans. George E. J. Powell and Eiríkur Magnússon (London: Richard Bentley, 1864), 24–27.

70: W.B. Yeats, *The Celtic Twilight* (Dublin: Maunsel and Co., 1905), 7.

THE MELANCHOLY QUOTIENT

86: Andrew Wawn, trans., "The Saga of the People of Vatnsdal," *The Sagas of Icelanders* (New York: Viking, 1997) 216–229.

91: Gunnar Karlsson, *A History of Iceland* (Minneapolis: University of Minnesota Press, 2000), 89–186.

105: Wallace Stevens, "Sunday Morning," *The Collected Poems of Wallace Stevens* (New York: Vintage Books, 1990), 66–71.

MINNEOTA: THE EARLY YEARS

125: W. H. Auden, "In Memory of W. B. Yeats," *Selected Poems*, ed. Edward Mendelson (New York: Vintage Books, 1979), 82.

126: William Stafford, "At the Un-National Monument along the Canadian Border," *The Way It Is* (St. Paul: Graywolf Press, 1998), 56.

126: David Ignatow, *Rescue the Dead* (Middletown: Wesleyan University Press, 1968), 44.

127: Robert Bly, "The Teeth Mother Naked at Last," *Eating the Honey of Words* (New York: HarperFlamingo, 1999), 76–77.

SILENCE AND NOISE

136: Johan Wolfgang von Goethe, *Selected Poetry of Johann Wolfgang von Goethe*, trans. David Luke (London: Penguin Books, 2005), 35.

137: Lawrence, "The White Horse," *The Complete Poems of D.H. Lawrence*, 683.

137: Bly, "Watering the Horse," *Eating the Honey of Words*, 26.

143: Louis Simpson, "The Silent Piano," *Owner of the House: New Collected Poems, 1940–2001* (Rochester: BOA Editions, 2003), XX.

147: Mark Crispin Miller, "Big Brother is You, Watching," *Boxed In: The Culture of TV* (Evanston: Northwestern University Press, 1988), 285–331.

A GIFT OF HORSES

161: Hasse and Barbro Schröeder, *Iceland: More Than Sagas* (Sweden: Schroders Ord & Bildbyra AB, 1990), 203.

163: Walt Whitman, "Song of Myself," *Leaves of Grass*, (New York: Bantam Classics, 1983), sec. 13.

165: Viðar Hreinsson, Andvökuskáld, (Reykjavik: Bjartur, 2003), 303.

168: James Wright, "A Blessing," *Collected Poems* (Middletown: Wesleyan University Press, 1971), 135.

169: Herman Pálsson, trans., *Hrafnkel's Saga and Other Icelandic Stories* (Middlesex: Penquin Books, 1971), 38-43.

CHRISTIANITY UNDER THE GLACIER

175: W.H. Auden and Louis MacNeice, *Letters from Iceland* (New York: Random House, 1969), 139 and 192.

177: Karlsson, *A History of Iceland*, 42.

186: Auden and MacNeice, *Letters from Iceland*, 138.

THE HOME OF POETRY

198: Kristján Árnason, "The Woman Who Passed a Moment Ago" and "In the Mountains," trans. Wincie Jóhannsdottir.

199: Árnason, "Autumn," trans. Wincie Jóhannsdottir, Margret Arnar, and Bill Holm.

200: Robert Bly, "Listening," *The Night Abraham Called to the Stars* (New York: HarperCollins, 2001), 91.

FOG

208: Auden and MacNeice, *Letters from Iceland*, 8.

210: George Bernard Shaw, *Heartbreak House* (London: Penguin Books (Dover Publications), 2000) 65.

BILL HOLM was born in 1943 on a farm north of Minneota, Minnesota. He continues to live in Minnesota half the year while he teaches at Southwest State University in Marshall. He spends summers at his little house on a North Iceland fjord where he writes, practices the piano, and waits for the first dark after three months of daylight. He is the author of eleven books, both poetry and essays. His most recent poetry book is *Playing the Black Piano* (Milkweed Editions, 2004).

More Books from Bill Holm

To order books or for more information,
contact Milkweed at (800) 520-6455
or visit our Web site (www.milkweed.org).

Eccentric Islands:
Travels Real and Imaginary

 Eccentric Islands is a literary expedition across the map to islands both real and imaginary. Like a modern-day literary Darwin, Bill Holm travels physically to Isla Mujeres, Molokai, Iceland, Madagascar, Mallard Island, and mentally to The Necessary Island of the Imagination, the Piano Island, and the acute isolation of the Island of Pain. Holm introduces beguiling characters and cultures, from the well-read radio man on an Icelandic freighter to the Robert Johnson of Madagascar and his instrument, the vahila. The result is a cultural stew pot where the ingredients get to swap flavors and make something new and strange.

"Magnificent. . . . Holm frames a deeply personal mythology, where the most important island is the one within us, the interior island of imagination and soul."—David Ulin, *L.A. Weekly*

"Holm is as philosophical as her is descriptive, as funny as he is feisty. . . . Vibrant, adventurous, and empathetic, Holm relishes the uniqueness of each place."—Donna Seaman, *Booklist*

"Like a modern-day Thoreau, Holm convincingly 'downsize[s] the universe in order to get a better look at it.' These essays are replete with pith and humor."—*Publishers Weekly* (starred review)

Coming Home Crazy:
An Alphabet of China Essays

A captivating journey through contemporary China. With Holm as companion, one learns what it is like to travel by "hard-seat" train to a remote village, to smuggle Chinese classics back into China, and to experience Mickey Mouse-mania in the Middle Kingdom. A literal alphabet of essays, with at least one essay for each letter, this book offers the first Icelandic-Lutheran-Minnesotan analysis of one of the most enigmatic countries in the world.

"[A] fantastic expedition into the whims, absurdities, smells, tastes and wonders of modern Chinese life. . . . Holm provides a warm, wise and unrelentingly witty guide to surviving China."—*San Diego Magazine*

"Entertaining, thought-provoking and touching. After reading his book, you won't look at the United States or China the same way."—*Philadelphia Inquirer*

"The warmth, courage and enduring spirit of the Chinese people permeate the pages of Coming Home Crazy."—*Charleston News and Courier/Evening Post*

The Heart Can Be Filled Anywhere on Earth

Bill Holm's postcard from home: Minneota, Minnesota. Investigating—through the lens of small-town life—what community means to us and the rigid definitions we give to "success" and "failure," Holm plumbs the depths of one's home place.

Growing up, Bill Holm could define failure easily; it was "to die in Minneota." But when he returned to his hometown twenty years later, stepping out of the mainstream into what others regard as a backwater, Holm began to question the pace of our culture and how, in the rush to get ahead, we've lost our roots.

"The tallest radical humorist in the Midwest and a truthful and graceful writer."—Garrison Keillor

"Bill Holm's is a classic American voice, but of a kind we haven't often heard lately. It's the voice of the prairie radical, the village agnostic, toting volumes of Walt Whitman . . . as he saunters through Minneota, Minnesota."—*Los Angeles Times*

"A fine writer with a wry, self-deprecating style, Holm has done what many authors aspire to do: make the dead live again." —*Library Journal*

Playing the Black Piano

In *Playing the Black Piano* Holm, like a modern-day Walt Whitman bestriding America and the world, comments on the waywardness and promise of the human species. The poems here reflect Holm's time in Iceland (his ancestral home), his ongoing love affair with music, a friend's death from AIDS, and his bold reactions to the world around him. Moving from Oregon forests to the deserts around Tucson, from the endless marketing of long-distance telephone service to the experience of undergoing an MRI, the poems speak of this man's full embrace of the world and his passion for living well.

"Bill Holm is not only one of the finest poets in North America, but (let me not mince words) he is now expressing his view of the world in the finest poems he has ever written."—Eric Friesen, *Star Tribune*

"Holm is a musician as well as a poet. He fills his work with wonderful music, and with snapshots of his travels. . . . We flip past Iceland to China, the Dakotas, Greece, Alaska, Madagascar and Manhattan . . . by the time we reach the book's title poem, Death comes in a flurry, as Holm plays preludes and fugues, such as Mozart, Brahms and Beethoven."—*Philadelphia Inquirer*

Milkweed Editions

Founded in 1979, Milkweed Editions is one of the largest independent, nonprofit literary publishers in the United States. Milkweed publishes with the intention of making a humane impact on society, in the belief that good writing can transform the human heart and spirit. Within this mission, Milkweed publishes in four areas: fiction, nonfiction, poetry, and children's literature for middle-grade readers.

Join Us

Milkweed depends on the generosity of foundations and individuals like you, in addition to the sales of its books. In an increasingly consolidated and bottom-line-driven publishing world, your support allows us to select and publish books on the basis of their literary quality and the depth of their message. Please visit our Web site (www.milkweed.org) or contact us at (800) 520-6455 to learn more about our donor program.

Interior design by Wendy Holdman
Typeset in Warnock Pro
by Prism Publishing Center
Printed on acid-free Rolland Enviro
(100% postconsumer waste) paper
by Friesens

Skagafjörður

Skagi

Keta

Skagaströnd

Húnaflói

Þverárfjall

Blönduós

Langidá

Húnafjörður

Bland

Hrútafjörður

Miðfjörður

Vatnsdalur

Hof